A QUILLWORK COMPANION
AN ILLUSTRATED GUIDE TO TECHNIQUES OF PORCUPINE QUILL EMBROIDERY

by

Jean Heinbuch

Eagle's View Publishing Company
6756 North Fork Road
Liberty, UT 84310

ISBN: 0-943604-25-7 in Paperback
ISBN: 0-943604-26-5 in Hardback
Library of Congress Catalog Card Number: 90-82648

FIRST EDITION

TABLE OF CONTENTS

TABLE OF ILLUSTRATIONS

EMBARKATION

I saw my first piece of porcupine quill embroidery in a primitive art collection belonging to a friend in 1972. It seemed quite an oddity, but immediately captured my attention; I was nineteen years old at the time and already very involved with sewing. One of my university minors was theatrical costuming, my major was art and I was adding to my funds for these studies with embroidery done for a local needlework shop. The seeds were sown on fertile ground, to say the least, and the rest was left to either mother nature or human nature. To this day, I'm not sure which.

Keeping my eyes and ears open, I hoped to discover clues as to how quill embroidery was done but for two years had no luck. Then in 1974 I began to meet people who had at least heard of the art form. I found a source of porcupine quills (no mean trick in Illinois in the early '70s) and wonder of wonders, a book that illustrated the many techniques involved in porcupine quill embroidery. I assumed all would be downhill from this point, which was a lucky thing, indeed. Fourteen years later, in hindsight, I think I might never have started the project if I had then realized the magnitude of the undertaking.

By 1976 I was sitting in my tipi under a tall, ponderosa pine tree, on the West Fork of the Bitterroot River, with all of my materials laid out around me, embarking on a voyage of discovery that will, to all appearances, endure for the remainder of my life. That first piece of quillwork was never finished. I started with an improper backing material (in that case, coarse canvas) and at a skill level that was far beyond me. However, I learned so much that it whetted my appetite for more and I knew that I was hooked.

In time I learned. It is not necessary to cut porcupine quills off a dried hide with an exacto blade. Never boil quills. Twisting a thread just so will magically turn a quill this way or that. No matter the cost, brain-tanned leather is THE material to quill on, and the real milestone in my work was reached the day I learned to tan my own leather. This last has been so important to me that I now realize it should have been the first skill I learned. Hind sight again.

It has taken me years to reach what I think is an advanced skill level. This has, in large part, been due to the lack of information available on the art of porcupine quill embroidery. Until just a few years ago the only printed material available of any quality was contained in the standard text on the subject written by William C. Orchard in 1916, entitled *The Technique of Porcupine Quill Decoration Among the Indians of North America* (available from Eagle's View Publishing). While this is an excellent volume and a must for any quillworker's library, it falls short of explaining how the various techniques are rendered useable. In this book, I hope to fill the gap that has existed between cerebral and practical knowledge on the subject that I hold dearest to my heart - that of porcupine quill embroidery.

I have skipped historical background in this endeavor, as that has been admirably covered by other authors and, for the most part, I have concentrated my efforts on learning skills at the expense of being less than expert on history and design dispersal. There is, however, a brief bibliography at the end of the book for those interested in pursuing these subjects. One other subject that will be noticeably absent in this volume is a discussion on cultural mores and customs concerning quillwork. Even should I know much on the subject, it is not a proper subject for a general audience as it deals with matters of great importance to those involved. Light-handed scattering of half-truths are abusive and offensive to many whom I hope will find this book a useful tool.

I wish to extend special thanks to David Lehto and George Dudley for taking time from their busy schedules to photograph items from their collections for inclusion in this book, and extra special thanks to Michael Rider for lending his time and skills in taking the black and white photographs of my quillwork presented in this book. Also, I wish to express my appreciation to Brenda Martin, Winona Whitney and Kris Sweat for proofing the manuscript.

In closing, I would like to dedicate this book to the Lizard, for without his help it would not have been.

Chapter I
INTRODUCTION

How to Use This Book

Each of the techniques illustrated and explained in this book builds on those previously given. In other words, to keep repetition to a minimum, new steps are explained in detail the first time they are used and it is assumed that those steps are understood for future techniques. What this all means is that the book should be read from the beginning and each technique understood before going on to the next one. Even if a particular technique is not

actually used, the section should be read just in case an innovation is presented that might be needed in future techniques.

Keep in mind that the beginning techniques are extremely important to master and should be practiced at great lengths so that the ideas presented in those chapters are completely understood. This will prevent a great deal of frustration as the quillworker works through the later chapters in the book.

All of the quillwork shown in the following pages was created by the author in an effort to assure the reader that the directions given in each section are accurate and will really work out into the specific technique discussed; hopefully, with a minimum of effort and thought on the craft worker's part.

Quill Preparation

Let us begin at the beginning. To do porcupine quill embroidery it is necessary to find a source of quills. Quills are available from many mail order Indian craft stores. The main drawback to this source is that one cannot choose the quills desired and many times quills are shipped that are suited mainly for stringing earrings; many of these outlets do, however, offer whole porcupine hides. Another source is the local hide dealer. He may not have any porcupine hides in stock, but can help locate someone who does. In any event, from whatever source, get the largest hide possible as they will have the extra long, slim quills that are preferable for the majority of the quillwork techniques taught in this book.

7

People lucky enough to live in the "porcupine belt," have another main source. Late every summer, porcupines follow some kind of migration pattern and many meet their end on highways. They are also highly visible at this time and many are shot by ardent tree protectors. As word gets around that there is a use for the quills, many of these unfortunate animals will end up on your porch. Hopefully most of them will be in a lesser state of decay. Keep in mind that the quills may be in your mouth for a short period as the work progresses and avoid over-heated animals. Aside from the nasty task of fighting various creepy crawlies for the quills from rotted carcasses, too much heat forces the grease from the hide into the quills and this ruins the quills. Do not be put off by all this gruesomeness, however; dead porcupines are the main source of quills available today.

It might be appropriate to discuss the pros and cons of actually killing a porcupine to procure the quills. There really isn't much that can be said in favor of the practice and it is very much like a farmer killing his cow to get a bucket of milk. There are available "road kills," hide dealers, mail order outlets and it is even possible to obtain quills from live porcupines. In the latter case, over the years the story has circulated that a towel or burlap bag can be thrown over the porcupine and the quills that adhere to it removed. This can be done, but all that is collected is the coarsest grade of quills which, for the most part, will be unsuitable for good work.

Another method of obtaining quills from a live porcupine is effective but entails a certain amount of danger and cannot be recommended. Still, the process is described below as it is interesting and is one that the author has observed: Plucking a live porcupine is a two man (or two woman) job. It is not for the faint of heart. First, the porcupine must be persuaded to quit waddling around in the brush. Generally, if a porcupine is followed closely enough he will halt and tuck his nose to his belly and bristle the quills on his back and tail;

this is a warning to leave him alone. It looks fearsome, but what must be watched for is a swatting motion made with the tail. An accepted fable is that porkies can shoot their quills; this is nonsense. But, they can move their tail so fast that it is very difficult to see and it is this habit that makes the next step dangerous. With this method a person located behind the porky claps their hands or stomps their feet and when the porky lifts his tail to line up on the intruder, that person quickly grabs the tail and jerks him off his feet and into the air. The quills on the top of the tail all lay in one direction (from the base of the tail pointing toward the tip) and the bottom of the tail is covered with harmless bristles, so that when the animal is lifted off his feet by the tail, the quills are rendered harmless by gravity and the animal's own weight. Those who practice this technique do not use gloves as it inhibits their grip and quills tend to become embedded in the fabric. Once they have a firm grip on the tail, a partner plucks quills as quickly as possible. A person's arms tire quickly from the weight, and the animal must be given a rest from the head-down position every ten minutes or so. There is a large vein running through his skull to his teeth and it is possible to harm him by hanging him upside down for too long.

The quills that are most useful lie across the shoulders and down the sides toward the flanks and the number of good quality quills varies from animal to animal. On some, the long slim quills run quite far back toward the tail; on others, they coarsen halfway down the back. In any event, those who pluck live porkies are careful not to put too large a hole in his defenses. Another danger with this method is that the porcupine may try to grab a person's arm with his back feet when he is held upside down. He must be prevented from doing this as he will use this additional leverage to swing back and bite his captor. You may be assured that his front incisors are no joke.

When plucking quills from dried hides, soak the hide in a bucket of water for a day. The quills will pull easily from the soaked hide. The most useful quills are located across the shoulders and along the sides. Become familiar with the locations of the different lengths and widths of quills on the first few hides or carcasses handled. Completely strip each hide even though some of the sizes are seldom needed for the embroidery as it seems a waste not to, and there always seems to be someone who can use them. The very coarse quills are used in making earrings and the very finest quills are best for plaiting, though a few of these will cover an amazing amount of space. The guard hair (long hair that lays over the quills) of the porcupine is used in making dance roaches and the bristly underside of the tail may be made into an old-style hair brush. There need actually be very little waste if you are careful.

As the porcupine is plucked, it is best to keep the various size quills separated and every quillworker develops a favorite method of sorting quills. If a lot of quilling is planned, large quantities of quills need to be dyed at the same time. It seems best, under these circumstances, to only do a general sorting at the time of the plucking. Place the coarsest quills in one pile, the finest in another and the general work quills in yet another. If guard hair is also pulled, keep it in a nice bundle by itself. On the other hand, to do only a small amount of quillwork, it will be best to spend more time on sorting. Try to locate quills of the same length and width, make small piles and keep them separate all through the washing and dying processes.

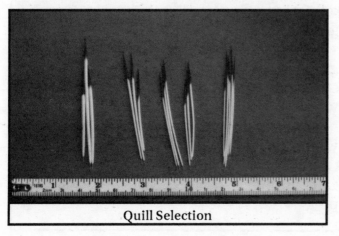

Quill Selection

Study the quills in the Photograph (bottom left). The coarsest ones on the left will be excellent for making earrings, necklaces and such where the quill is strung on a thread, but they are very difficult to sew neatly on to leather. It is very tempting to the beginning quillworker to use these, as an area can be filled quickly, but only an experienced quillworker can hope to make these quills behave properly, and even then the work looks as coarse as the quills used. It cannot be stated strongly enough that it is really best to forget about using this type of quill for embroidery work.

The next three groups of quills (to the right of the coarse quills) are what you will want for general embroidery work, wrapping and weaving. The shorter ones came from smaller animals and the longer ones from larger animals. The shorter quills work fine, but there will be more splicing involved and this will slow the work down somewhat. They are, however, more commonly available so it may be best to get used to dealing with them. The only techniques where it is essential to have the extra long quills are the multiple quill, wide-row bands in the advanced techniques section of this book.

The group of quills on the far right side of Photo (left) are the extra fine variety. These are primarily used for plaited quillwork. It is possible to plait with a coarser quill but again, the work will suffer. Always keep in mind that the object is to do the best possible quillwork and, though it may not seem so at first, handling a finer quill will always be easier than using a coarse one.

After plucking and the initial sorting, it is time to wash the quills. Porcupines are extremely greasy animals and the quills are coated with grease and dirt. This must all be stripped off of the quill before dyeing. To do so, fill a dish pan with warm water and add a mild soap with a small amount of chlorine bleach. The bleach is used to somewhat disinfect the quills, but using too much can damage them, so be sure to use a light hand when adding it to the water.

Allow the quills to soak in the soapy water for a few minutes and then stir them around with a slotted strainer spoon to remove all of the dirt. When they are clean, pour the water off through a colander, place the quills back in the pan and rinse with cool water. Repeat the rinsing procedure until all of the soap is gone. Let the quills drain in the colander for half an hour and then either spread them on a tray to dry or they may be dyed at this time.

By nature, quills resist dyeing. Most of the secrets of old-time dye recipes have disappeared long ago and are just now being rediscovered. For the beginner, it is far simpler to rely on modern dye materials and concentrate on learning to mix these into approximations of old colors. A few modern dyes are, by themselves, capable of copying old colors and the rest can be adjusted with a splash of this and a dash of that. **Table I** will give the reader some ideas on how to create old-time colors, but this is really fun to play around with, so by all means experiment.

A small list of old time dyes is located at the end of the book in **Appendix B** for those interested in pursuing this area of study. At the present time there is a controversy over when commercial dyes were actually in common use among quillworkers. The Fur Trade Museum in Chadron, Nebraska ran a sample of quillwork, known to have been made in the early 1850s, through an F.B.I. lab test. They found that the quills had been dyed entirely with commercially prepared dyes. This dependence on commercial dyes may indicate a much earlier usage and quillworkers who prefer to rely on modern dyes need feel no sense of guilt in doing so.

As explained above, the quills must be dampened before the dyeing proceeds. If they are fresh from the washing procedure they are ready to go into the dye pot; if not, put the quills into a pan of warm water and allow them to soak for a few minutes. Then drain them in a

Table I

Old-Time Color	Dye Combination
Red	scarlet and chestnut brown
	scarlet and dark brown
	scarlet, tangerine and dark brown
Light Blue	navy blue (leave in dye bath a short time)
	royal blue and chestnut brown
Blue	denim blue, chestnut brown and kelly green
Green	jade green
	forest green and chestnut brown
	jade green and scarlet
Purple	garnet and navy blue
Yellow	yellow gold and gold
	gold
	yellow gold and yellow
Black	black and navy blue
	black and purple
Pink	rose pink

colander until the dye bath is ready.

The following directions for dyeing quills assume that quite a bit of quillwork is going to be done and are given for gallon-sized batches of quills. If the reader plans to do small projects and will not need large amounts of a single color, it will be necessary to decrease the given amounts of water and dye.

Place two or more gallons of water (do not exceed three gallons) in a large enamel pot or pan. A large enamel wash basin is a good choice. Put the pan on the stove and heat the water to just below the boiling point. It is very important not to get the water too hot as this will make the quills brittle and difficult to work with. Put a pint of hot water in a glass jar and stir the dyes into the water until they dissolve. Then, pour the dye solution into the water in the pan and stir again. Place the quills in the hot dye and stir gently to immerse the quills in the solution. Quills float, so it is necessary to periodically stir and turn the quills or the top ones will not dye as darkly as the submerged ones. Keep the dye solution just below the boiling point. The heat is necessary for good color penetration. It generally takes at least forty-five minutes for the dye to penetrate the quills and some colors will take longer.

In some areas of the country it may be necessary to add vinegar to the dye solution to get the colors to set in the quills. It will be worth trying this once or twice to see if it makes any difference in the quality of the finished product. Half of a cup or less should be plenty for the quantity of dye solution discussed in these directions.

When the proper shade is attained, strain the quills out of the dye by pouring the solution through the colander. Rinse the quills with warm water until little dye is coming out of them. Keep in mind that the quills may be held in your mouth and be sure to rinse thoroughly so that the dye won't come off of them at that point in the work. Allow the quills to drain for a while and then spread them on a tray to dry. Store in a covered container.

The best surface to work on when doing traditional quill embroidery is brain-tanned leather. Aside from being more "authentic" than other materials, the main reason for using it instead of commercially prepared skins, is that during the tanning process the hide fibers are left intact. The fibers are broken and short in commercial leather and will not hold the tiny surface stitches a quillworker should use. It is possible to stitch all of the way through commercial leather, but this is extremely tedious and makes fine work very difficult.

The making of brain-tanned leather is covered in **Appendix A** and serious quillworkers will want to learn how to tan their own hides. A good brain-tanned hide is very expensive and buying them may limit the amount of work that can be done. Besides, it is very satisfying to have complete control over your materials and ultimately, the finished product.

Tools

There are a small number of tools that

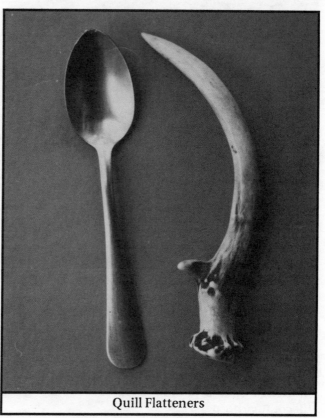

Quill Flatteners

11

are necessary for porcupine quill embroidery. The following list and accompanying photographs should cover everything needed to get started:

Needles: The size of the needle used is a matter of individual choice. I prefer to use a size 12 sharps beading needle. Do not use too coarse a needle or the work will suffer.

Thread and Beeswax: The beginning quillworker should start with a size A, O or OO Nymo beading thread. Actually, a fine cotton or silk thread (size A or B) is the best, but these tend to fray and break, and can be frustrating for the novice. All of these threads should be waxed prior to use. A fine thread made of sinew that has been soaked and rolled is a nice touch for "traditional" pieces but using this will slow the work considerably and only more advanced quillworkers will want to use this material.

Quill Flatteners: These come in all

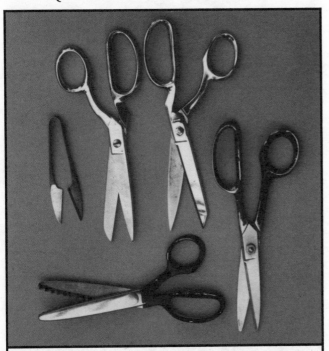

This selection of scissors should cover most needs. The pair on the left are a modern-made set of bonsai shears that is an exact replica of shears made as early as the 1700s. The center two pairs are general purpose sewing shears. One pair has a knife edge and the other has a serrated edge. The pair on the right will handle the heaviest of leather and on the bottom is a pair of pinking shears for the making of decorative borders.

shapes and sizes. A stainless steel teaspoon works well and is available everywhere. A polished antler tip works very well (See Photo on Page 11). If bone or antler flatteners are used, be sure the burnishing side (the side used to flatten quills) is smooth, as the slightest roughness can damage the quills.

Rulers and Compass: Keep a variety of ruler sizes. A six inch, twelve inch and yardstick make up a good selection. The compass need not be anything too fancy.

Scissors: These are a matter of personal preference. For the actual quillwork only one pair is needed but for the construction involved in various pieces, a variety is necessary. Notable among these are leather shears, pinking shears and extra good fabric shears.

Marking Pens: Use extra fine tip marking pens for laying out quilling patterns on the leather. Any color is fine, but brown is the easiest to erase from smoked leather if a mistake is made. Be sure the ink is indelible or it will smear as you work. An emery file or piece of sandpaper may be used to scratch out incorrect lines.

Awls: Most of the awls a quillworker will use are for general, constructive sewing, but they are included in this list of tools as they are necessary for quillwork done on birch bark and, also, if the quillworker wishes to try old-time techniques without needles. Quilling on birch bark requires an awl that is extremely fine. A small glover's needle set into a handle is about the right size. The three cornered hole that such a tool makes is preferable to a round hole. Sewing quills with an awl and sinew will need a slightly larger awl. This process is speeded considerably by the use of a bone needle; the size of the needle will determine the size awl to use.

Masking Tape: This is used as a backing for the leather to prevent it from stretching as the work progresses.

In addition to the above, some or all of the following tools will be needed for the actual construction of the articles that will be quilled.

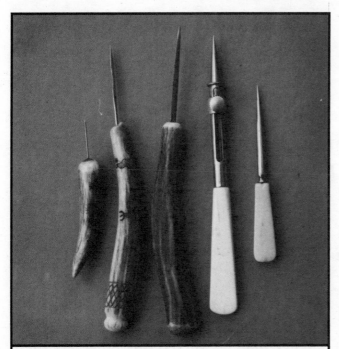

The awls shown here specialize in different jobs. The fine, three cornered awl on the left is made of a glovers needle and is used in birch bark quill work to poke holes in the bark for the quills. The two awls to the right of it are larger three cornered awls for sewing on leather with sinew. The two awls on the right come to round, tapered points and are used to punch holes in leather for lacing and thongs.

on the left is for birch bark quilling, the one beside it for sewing quills with an awl and sinew and the others for general sewing), and an assortment of scissors that are indispensable (the set on the left are modern bonsai shears that are a good reproduction of old time scissors, then a large set of shears with a serrated edge for trimming quill tips, next a set of sharp fabric shears, heavy leather shears and finally a set of pinking shears for decorative edging).

Antler awl, bone needle, sinew and obsidian finger knife.

Several sizes of round tipped and three cornered tipped (called sharps and glover's, respectively) needles are commonly used. Use the smaller sized (#6 - #8) glover's needles. Also, heavy duty (size D to F) sewing threads, craft knives, large awls (both round and three cornered tipped) and a pair of needle-nosed pliers.

Shown in Photographs on Pages 11, 12 and 13 are my favorite quill flatteners, a selection of quilling and sewing awls (the fine one

Chapter II
GENERAL WORK INSTRUCTIONS AND BASIC STITCHES

When a person makes the decision to learn quillwork, he or she usually has a specific project in mind. If this is the first quillwork attempted, keep the design simple and the piece fairly small. Learning quillwork takes quite a bit of time and it is not desirable to have to spend an entire year or two on the first project. It is best not to attempt rosettes and curved lines when first starting. If the work is kept to straight row work for the first few pieces it will be possible to concentrate on learning to handle the quills with some degree of dexterity. When the quillworker feels competent with straight rows, it is best to practice varying the width of the rows, tapering to points and widening the rows into hourglass shapes. With a little diligent practice it will not be too long before one can feel comfortable working in the tight circles required in rosette work.

Before beginning to quill, the selected pattern must be drawn on the leather (a few simple designs are shown in **Table II**). The quillwork will be done on the grain side of the leather, so at this time flip the hide over and put masking tape on the flesh side over the area that will be quilled. This will stiffen the leather slightly and prevent it from stretching and moving while the work is done on the other side. Return to the grain side and draw the guidelines to the pattern on the leather with an indelible marking pen. Be sure to keep the lines straight. The quillwork will follow these lines exactly and will not be any straighter than the guidelines.

As a general rule, the guide lines in the rows of the pattern should be 3/8" or less apart.

This will allow at least two or three passes across the row with each quill. There are a few exceptions to this rule and they are noted in the sections covered by those particular techniques.

The next thing that must be done is the final sorting of the quills. Decide on the size and length to be worked with and place these quills in a small pile. Save any coarser and finer quills in separate piles and discard the remaining hair and broken quills. Finally, use a pair of scissors to snip the barbed ends from the quills that will be used.

The quills must be softened just prior to use and there are basically two methods to do this: (1) The traditional method is to place a small bundle of quills (with the barbs removed) in the quillworker's mouth. Only a few quills are kept in the mouth at one time as they can swell a little too much if they remain there too long. It is surprising how much help the tongue gives in maneuvering the quills around and this can save time. Still, this method has some danger and if the reader chooses to use it they do so at their own risk. (2) The quills may be placed in a bowl of warm water to soak for a

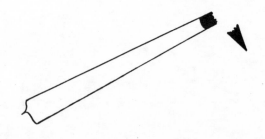

Remove the barb from the Quill

14

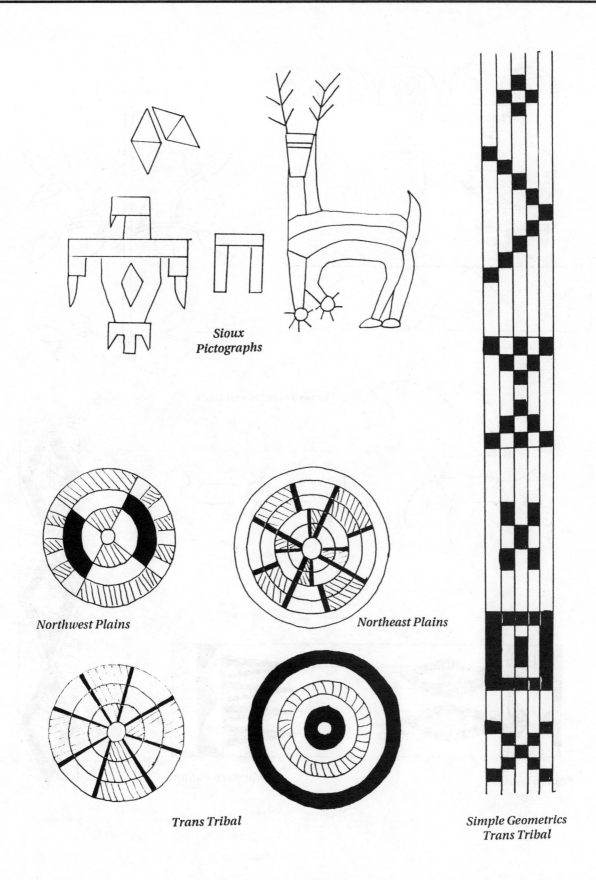

*Sioux
Pictographs*

Northwest Plains

Northeast Plains

Trans Tribal

*Simple Geometrics
Trans Tribal*

Table II

Great Lakes Line Work

Midwest Line Work

Trans Tribal Line Work

Trans Tribal Floral Work

Eastern Sioux

Northern Plains

Midwest

Table II (Continued)

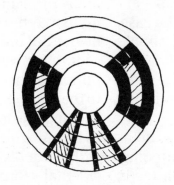

short period of time and then kept in a damp paper towel as the work continues. Keep in mind, however, that they will swell while in the towel and must be constantly watched. If, at any time, the quills seem rubbery and will not flatten properly, remove them from the towel and allow them to dry a bit. Swelled quills will never lie entirely flat. One way or the other, the quills must be softened just prior to working with them.

Everything is now ready to start quilling. The quills are soft and the pattern is drawn on the leather and in hand. Straight row work will require two needles - one to run along the top guideline and one to run along the bottom guideline. Do not put too long of a piece of thread on the needles as it could fray and break as a stitch is pulled tight. Fifteen to eighteen inches will usually hold up well. **Figure 1** shows how to knot the thread on the leather. This is

an old embroiderers' knot that stays on the surface of the work. Insert the needle at Point A and run it through to Point B, about a sixteenth of an inch away. Pull the thread through until just a bit of the end remains at Point A. (Note: As with all of the stitches in quillwork, the needle does not go through the leather but just under the surface as illustrated below). Re-insert the needle at Point A and have it exit the leather about halfway between Points A and B at Point C in Figure 1. Pull this stitch fairly snug but be careful not to put too much stress on it at this time. The next stitch in the knot begins by passing through the thread and then the leather at Point D. It exits at Point E and again catches the thread at Point F. Pull the stitch up securely as it will now tighten down firmly. Stitch to the starting point of the row and then knot the other thread in the same manner.

Before sewing the softened quills with the barb removed to the leather, each must be slightly flattened. The easiest method is to grasp the tip of the quill with your fingers and pull it through your teeth. This will eliminate

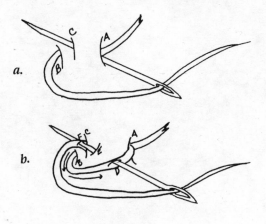

Figure 1

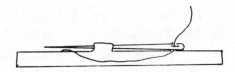

Needle passing through leather on a back stitch

the air in the quill and it should flatten nicely. If it doesn't seem to be flat, it may have absorbed too much moisture. If this is the case, allow the quills to dry a bit and they should work fine. It is important that the quills be flat or they will not present a smooth surface when the work is complete, even after burnishing with a quill flattener.

There are a couple of alternative methods that can be used in the initial flattening. Some people hold the quill tip in their teeth, pinch the quill with their fingernails and run the nails the length of the quill. This method works quite well. It is also possible to hold the quill in the fingers and run a fingernail the length of the quill as in the process above. This is a much slower process but does not necessitate placing the quill in the mouth.

Figure 2 illustrates the three stitches needed to do the quill techniques in this book. The most often used is the Backstitch and it allows the stitches to remain on the surface of the leather. Right-handed people will work the Backstitch from left to right; left-handed people will work to the reverse. The Horizontal Spot Stitch is used for the Sawtooth Single Thread Technique in the advanced techniques section and the Vertical Whip Stitch is used with some edging techniques.

The Backstitch is shown in Figure 2a. Point A is located at the place where the thread has emerged from the leather after the knot is made. The needle is inserted at Point B and again emerges at Point C. This forms the first stitch and it should be pulled snugly over the quill. Note that the needle, and consequently the thread as it follows through, stays to the upper most side of the thread as it comes out of Point A. This shows the stitching for the top of the row and it can be seen in the second half of the Figure that the thread loops <u>over</u> the previous stitch. This keeps the loops formed by the stitches to the outside of the row. As the stitches are very small and pulled tightly into the leather, this will in effect hide them and protect the thread from wear and tear. An examination of old quilled pieces will show that the threads in quillwork seldom give out. Whole sections of quills may be missing, as shown in in the photo below, but the stitching is still intact. The procedure is reversed for the stitching along the bottom of the row. Again, the loops are formed to the outside of the row. This time it is done by keeping the needle to the underside of Point A as it comes out of the leather. A little practice with the quills will show that if the loops are accidentally formed to the inside the thread will be exposed across the entire bottom of the quill as it passes on to the next stitch. This is a very common mistake made by the beginning quillworker.

Before beginning, it is important to know how to finish a row of quillwork. There will be exceptions to the method shown here and they will be treated individually with differing techniques as appropriate. For the most part, however, the method illustrated in **Figure 3** will be used. This entails simply folding the quill under itself, trimming the end and catch-

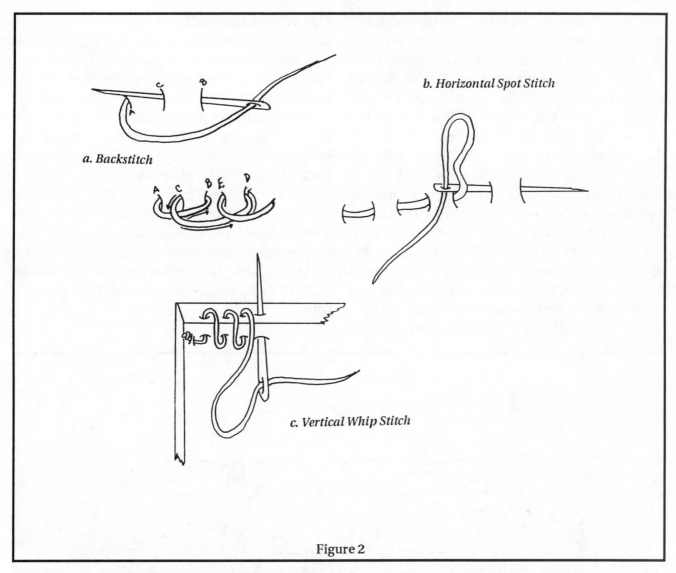

a. Backstitch

b. Horizontal Spot Stitch

c. Vertical Whip Stitch

Figure 2

ing a stitch over the loose end. This may seem a straight forward approach to a rather simple problem to the beginning quillworker, but getting the quill to fold under in an easy and quick maneuver has puzzled many modern quillworkers - including some of the best. The simple trick of twisting the thread, as shown in Figure 3, is all there is to it. As the twisted thread is pulled through the stitch it twists the quill around and under. Figure 3 illustrates this procedure step by step.

Figure 3a shows the quill already stitched to the bottom of the row. The quill has been folded to the top of the row and the crucial stitch is in progress. The thread enters and exits the leather in the normal backstitch, but the stitch is halted temporarily at this point

and the thread is looped over the quill clockwise. This is done by bringing the thread around the back of the quill and looping it across the front from the right side to the left and then crossing back again. Continue the stitch. As it pulls tight the quill will fold itself under. If it does not quite make it all the way, it is easy to twist it the rest of the way with your fingers. One other thing to watch for is the tendency for the top edge of the quill to pinch together instead of lying straight and flat. This is caused by the thread loop grabbing the quill too low. If this seems to be a problem, simply hold the thread a little higher on the quill as the stitch is pulled tight.

Figure 3b illustrates how the end of the quill is hidden at the end of the row. After

19

finishing the previous stitch, the thread at the top of the row is brought to a midway point in the row just under the final fold in the quill. Do this with a simple running stitch from the top of the row to the middle. Next, form a loop by stitching from the center of the row to the bottom. These stitches should all be hidden by the last fold in the quill. As the last stitch is pulled tight it is easy to see where the quill should be trimmed. It must be short enough so that it will not stick out from under the row of quillwork but long enough so that the stitch can be pulled taut without the thread slipping off of the end. Figure 3b shows the quill trimmed to a length that reaches about half way across the row. This should usually be about right.

The finished edge is shown in Figure 3c.

The end of the quill has been pulled neatly under, then stitched down. In Figure 3d the threads have been knotted off with three tiny backstitches. Though the stitches are easily seen in the Figure, in real life these should be so small that, unless it is known where to look for them, they cannot be seen. As there is no pressure on the stitching in quillwork the small backstitches will hold very well.

The row is finished in this Figure by working from the top of the row but this can also be done from the bottom of the row. This will be determined by how the quill lies at the end of the row. To tie off at the bottom, use the bottom thread and work towards the top of the row.

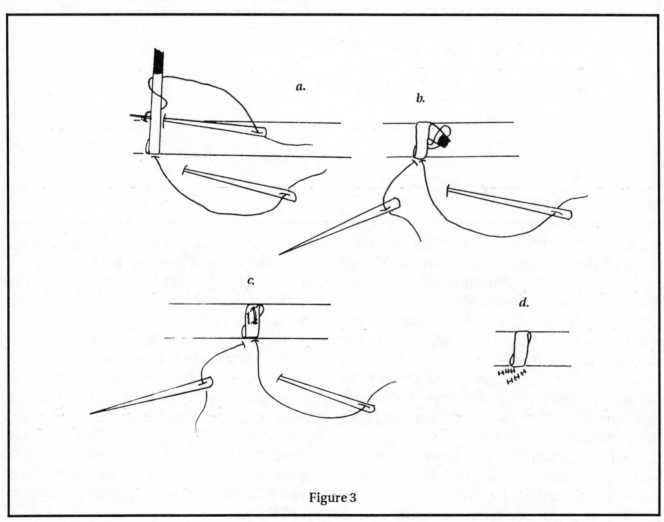

Figure 3

20

NOTES

Chapter III
BASIC QUILLING TECHNIQUES

Zigzag Technique

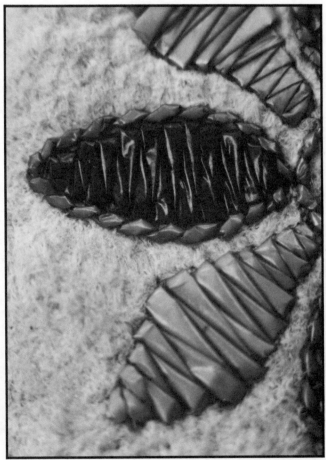

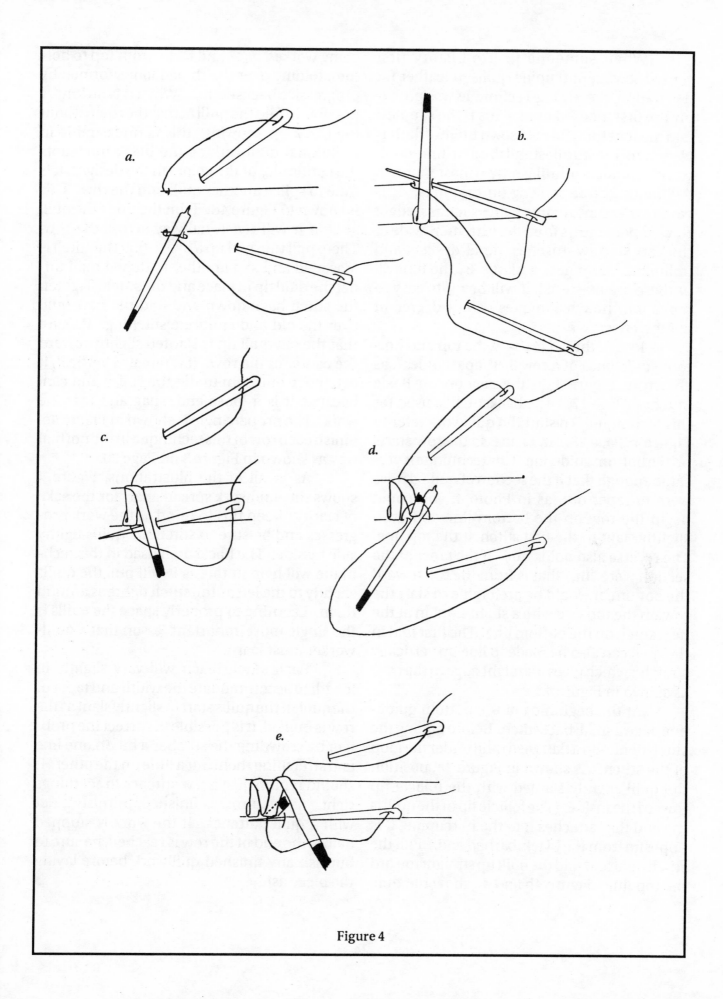

Figure 4

When someone in pre-history first started sewing porcupine quills to leather for decoration, the Zigzag Technique was probably the first method used. This is the simplest and most natural form of sewn quillwork. It is also one of the sturdiest and the first-time quill-worker should work diligently at mastering this technique before moving on to others. It is easily worked into many shapes such as straight rows, tapered rows from the extremely wide to the very narrow, rosettes, floral designs and unlimited curvilinear designs. By the time all of these are mastered, it will be quite easy to move into new techniques with a degree of competence.

Knot a thread on both the top and bottom guide lines of a row 3/8" apart or less, as shown in Figure 1 in the section on Basic Stitches (Page 17). The backstitch is used for this technique. To start the quillwork refer to **Figure 4** (Page 23). In Figure 4a the row starts on the bottom guideline. This technique is versatile enough that if the section of quilled rows were to taper out, as in Photo 4, you could begin the row on the bottom line and even slightly slant in the first stitch at the top line. The reverse also holds true. If the taper of the section were "in," that is from the top toward the bottom, it would be preferable to start the row on the top line with a slight slant in at the next stitch on the bottom line. The first fold in the quill can also be made to line up vertically straight, which gives a straight edge to the row, as shown in Figure 4.

At the beginning of the bottom guideline, take a small backstitch. Before pulling the stitch tight, slip a flattened quill under the loop of the stitch. As shown in Figure 4a, position the quill slightly slanted with the follicle tip toward the inside. (The follicle tip of the quill is the end that attaches it to the porcupine; it is opposite from the black, barbed end.) Pull the stitch tight and fold the quill up straight toward the top line. Figure 4b and 4c show the quill

being worked back and forth, from top to bottom, folding over the thread loops formed by progressive backstitches. When it is no longer possible to fold the quill across the row without the black tip showing (this is undesirable in traditional quillwork as the black interrupts the continuity of the colors in the design), it is time to splice another quill into the row. This is shown in Figure 4d. Trim the tip of the quill so that it will reach halfway across the row. Then, pull the quill up a bit, so that the stitch is loosened and slip another flattened quill under the quill tip in place and the stitch. Tighten the stitch back down and fold the new quill over the old and continue stitching. Be sure that the old quill tip is slanted slightly toward the center of the row. If it remains vertical, it can move out from under the splice and can, because it is a loose end, snag and tear the work. The proper angle is shown in Figure 4e. Finish each row of this technique in the normal way as shown in Figure 3 on Page 20.

As in all of the illustrations, Figure 4 shows the quillwork spread apart for the sake of clarity. Keep this in mind as the work progresses and be sure to stitch the quills tightly side by side. The backstitch used in this technique will help in this as it will pull the quills slightly to the left as the stitch tightens around them. Learning to properly space the quills is the single most important lesson that a quill-worker must learn.

Each stitch taken will vary slightly in length to accommodate the width and taper of the quill. If the quills start to slightly slant as the row is quilled, it is possible to correct the problem by crowding the stitches a bit on one line and stretching them out a little on the other. It should require just a few stitches to set things right. As each row is finished, burnish it flat with a quill flattener. If the work is stopped before the end of the row is reached, be sure to burnish any finished quillwork before laying the piece aside.

Simple Band Technique

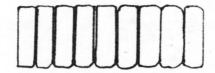

Simple Band quillwork has long been a hallmark of the accomplished quillworker. Its deceptively simple appearance belies the skill necessary to keep the work neat and the lines clean. No other technique will show flaws as readily as this one. The quillworker must pay strict attention to the details of the craft at all times when working this technique. Quills must be chosen for their similarity in width in

Close-up of Simple Band Technique. Note the similarity in the size of the quills which lends the technique important uniformity

each color that will be used and fairly fine quills should be avoided if possible; Simple Band work is not quite as strong as other forms of quillwork and a slightly larger quill will lend the work some additional strength. Do not, however, carry this to the extreme. A very coarse quill is hard to handle in this technique and will not flatten well.

Figure 5 illustrates the steps in the

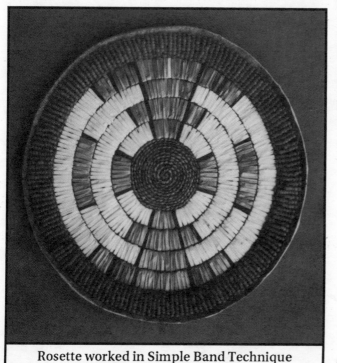

Rosette worked in Simple Band Technique
(edging is done in seed beads)

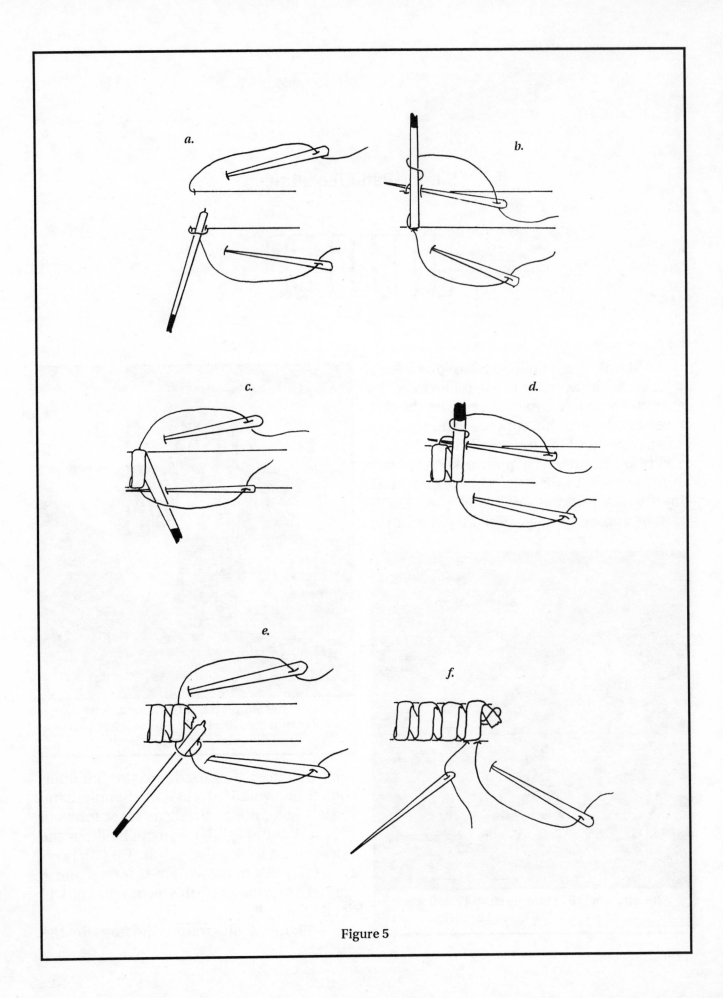

Figure 5

Simple Band Technique. The backstitch is used. Figure 5a shows the flattened quill being inserted under the first stitch on the bottom line. Actually the technique can be worked from either the bottom or top guideline, but the splices must be added from the same side on which the quillwork begins. Keep this in mind if working from the top and reverse the splices and finishing steps.

Illustrated in Figure 5b is the easiest and fastest method of working this technique. It can be seen that this is the same technique as used in the finishing method presented in Figure 3 (Page 20). The trick of twisting the thread around the quill to move it one way or the other will be used repeatedly throughout this book and it cannot be stressed strongly enough that this is a very important weapon in the quillworker's arsenal. In order to develop new techniques (or to redevelop old techniques, as is probably the case), one should constantly be aware of the interaction between the quills and the thread.

To get the quill to fold under itself, a clockwise loop of thread is placed around the quill after the needle has started the backstitch. Pull the needle through the leather and as the stitch is pulled tight, the thread will twist the quill under. In order to obtain a square and even top edge, hold the thread loop a little high on the quill as the stitch is pulled. This is easiest to accomplish with the nail on the thumb that holds the work, but it is really a matter of personal preference and the manner in which the work is held. Be sure not to hinder the folding movement of the quill. When the stitch is tight, it is simple to pull the excess quill through the stitch until the edge of the quill is even with the top guideline. It will be necessary to hold onto the thread as the quill is pulled to keep the stitch tight. Sometimes the thread will not twist the quill entirely into the proper position and this is corrected by finishing the fold under with the fingers. It is easy to manipulate the quill once the thread has started it into position.

Continue to quill the row as shown in Figure 5c and 5d. The bottom line is quilled with the backstitch alone and the top line will always employ a loop in the thread in addition to the backstitch; in the future this will be referred to as the "Looped Backstitch." It will be time to splice in a new quill when it is no longer possible for the quill to reach across the entire row without some of the black tip showing. The quill is trimmed off after the stitch on the top guideline as shown in Figure 5e. The next quill is added on the bottom line with just the backstitch. The quillwork continues this way to the end of the row and the last quill is finished in the normal way (See Figure 3, Page 20). Burnish the quillwork with a flattener as each row is finished. If the row is a fairly long one, it might be better to do this every couple of inches. It is important to keep this technique flat as the quills will appear neater and the work will be less subject to wear.

27

Single Thread Line Technique

This technique has many applications. It may be used to outline quilled areas, used alone as a single line or even used to completely fill an area. Select quills that are fairly fine when first practicing this technique. It is possible to use a bit thicker quill after the thread and quill manipulation is mastered, but do not use too thick of a quill at any time. They are too difficult to control in fine work like this and the final result will be messy. Do not flatten the quills in single quill line work until the line or area is finished. A flat quill will not pinch and turn under properly.

This technique begins by fastening the

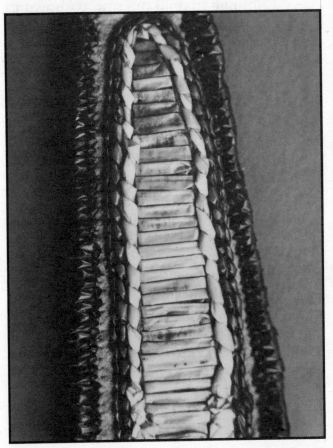

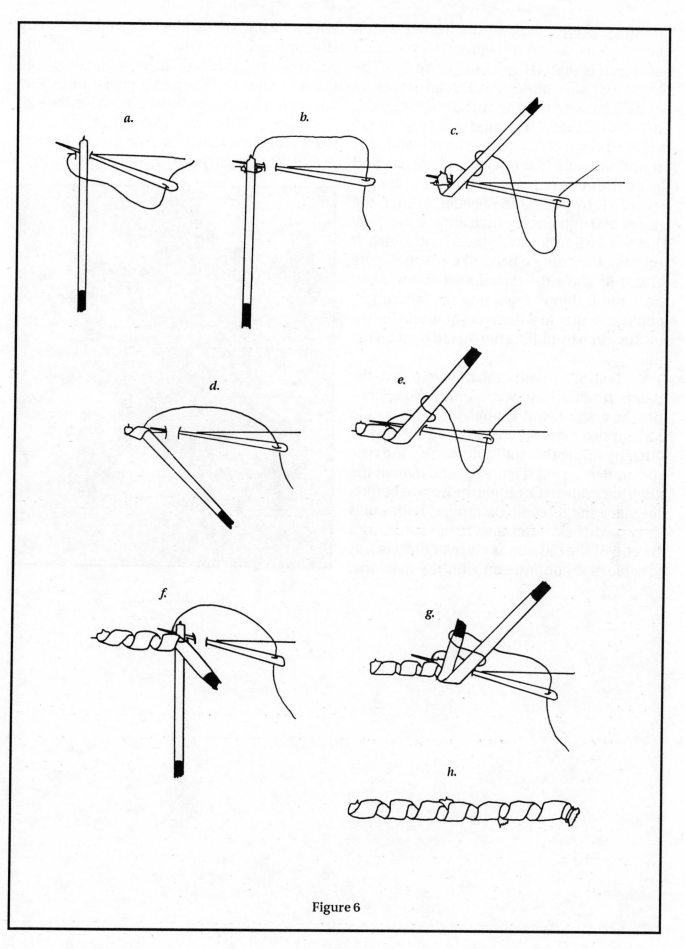

Figure 6

first <u>un-flattened</u> quill to the leather with a backstitch as shown in **Figure 6a**. A second backstitch is then taken as in Figure 6b. The needle remains under the thread (in other words, it comes up to the outside of the guide-line) so that it does not interfere as the thread is looped around the quill. The thread loops around the quill in a clockwise direction and the quill is folded up (Figure 6c). Continue the backstitch by pulling the needle through the leather and tighten the stitch around the quill. This will twist the quill under and pinch it somewhat creating a bead-like effect. Figure 6d and 6e show the technique continuing in the same fashion: Beginning the backstitch, looping the thread around the quill and finishing the stitch by pulling the thread tight on the quill.

Before the end of the colored part of the quill is reached, a new quill must be spliced into the work. Leave enough room on the old quill for two more stitches and loosen the last stitch by lifting the quill a little. Slip the new quill under the old (Figure 6g) and tighten the stitch back down. Continue the work as before, but place the thread loop around both quills for two stitches. After the second stitch, trim the end of the old one as close to the work as possible and continue on with the new one.

When the end of the line is reached, finish by stitching twice over the final quill. Pull the stitches very tight and trim the quill close to the thread. Knot the thread by taking three tiny backstitches in the leather as shown on Page 20 in Figure 3. Trim any ends sticking out of the work and then flatten the quillwork by burnishing thoroughly with a quill flattener.

Quill Wrapping Technique

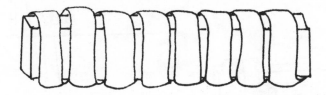

Quill Wrapping is one technique that requires little use of needle and thread and may be a good starting point for those would be quillworkers who have not yet developed their sewing skills. Just about anything that will hold still may be wrapped but in this Chapter on Basic Techniques we will focus on the most elementary form for use on leather thongs or

Quill Wrapping on rawhide

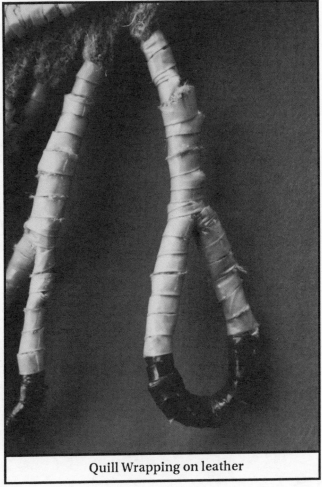

Quill Wrapping on leather

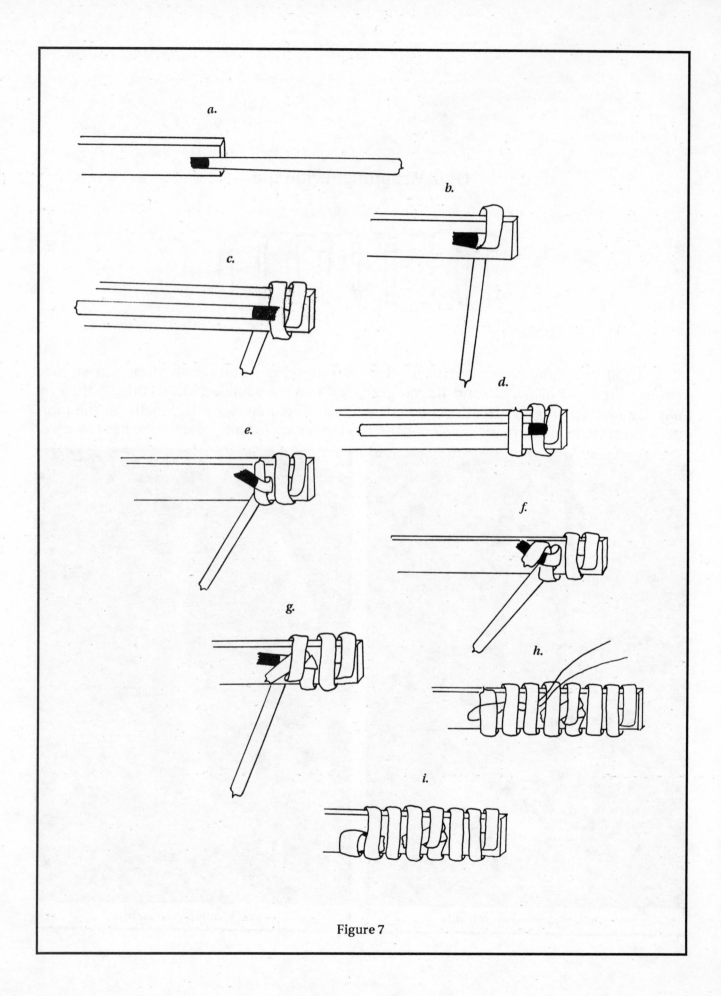

a.

b.

c.

d.

e.

f.

g.

h.

i.

Figure 7

rawhide slats. When cutting the rawhide or leather into strips, keep in mind the length of the quills and do not make the strips too wide (rawhide slats that are approximately 1/4" wide and leather thongs about 1/8" wide should do nicely). Ideally there should be at least two, and preferably three or more, wraps made with each quill. It is best to use a somewhat coarse quill if the wrapping is on rawhide slats and a bit finer quill with leather thongs.

Figure 7 is pretty much self-explanatory. To begin, the flattened quill is laid on the filler (thong or slat) as in Figure 7a. It is then folded up and over itself and around the filler (Figure 7b). The wrapping continues to the end of the quill and Figure 7c illustrates the beginning of the splice. Another flattened quill is laid on the filler. In Figure 7d the end of the old quill is folded up over the tip of the new quill. The tip is then folded over the old end. At this point, the remainder of the new quill will move to a more vertical position of its own accord and the old end is folded down over the tip of the new quill. Figure 7g illustrates the newly spliced quill folded up over the splice and on around the filler. There are several different methods to splice new quills into the work, but the one described here is the strongest and least likely to slip.

Continue to wrap quills around the filler to the end of the piece. One of the easiest methods of finishing wrapped work is to lay a thread loop under the last two or three wraps so that the loop sticks out of the end of the piece (Figure 7h). The loop is placed over the end of the last quill and slowly pulled back through the quill wraps. This will pull the end of the last quill under the final wraps and neatly secures the work.

Quill Plaiting Technique

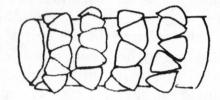

Plaited Quillwork is actually another form of the wrapping technique in that the finished quillwork is wrapped around an object. This method, however, is a much more versatile technique than the one explained in the last section. Plaiting makes it possible to wrap objects of widely varying sizes and shapes. Pipe stems, knife handles and pipe tampers are some of the most common items plaited, but quite often quill plaiting is also found on such unlikely objects as spoon handles, cylindrical objects of all kinds and porcupine tail hair brushes, to name just a few. Imagination is the only real limit to the use of this technique.

Plaited quillwork is accomplished by folding quills over and under two parallel threads held in the hands. The distance between the threads is determined by the width of the quills used, but should be between 1/12" and 1/16" apart. The threads must be very firmly held as the work progresses and a variety of techniques may be employed in order to keep tension on the thread. One is to roll two lengths of thread onto a half-inch dowel rod; be sure to roll enough thread on the dowel to do the entire piece without needing to splice more thread into the work. Then tie the dowel to the arms of your work chair so that it is positioned over your knees. It is possible to put tension on the dowel by holding it in place with the knees. When more thread is needed, all that is necessary is to release the knee pressure and the dowel is free to spin. The dowel may also be placed on the floor and held down with the feet and the pressure is relieved just as

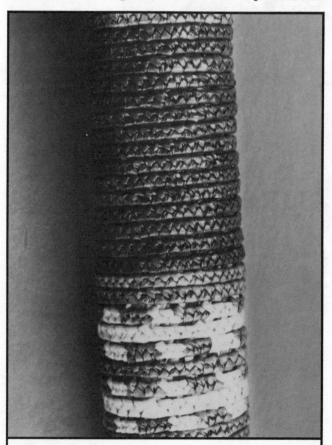

The use of fine quills will keep the plaiting tight

34

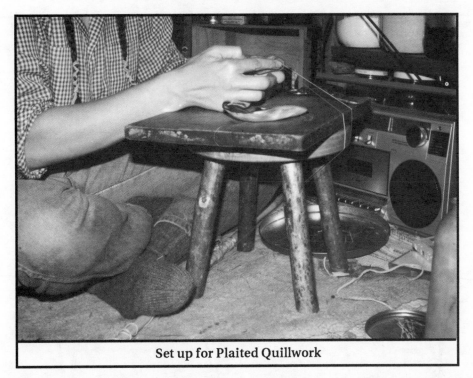

Set up for Plaited Quillwork

easily in this variation. An added advantage is that each foot can keep additional separate pressure on each thread. This is a help if the threads were not wound on the dowel with very even tension and as the work proceeds, one thread or the other unwinds slightly longer.

Another way to accomplish the same thing requires that the quillworker be seated on the floor. Roll the two lengths of thread on a short piece of half inch dowel (this piece of dowel need be no longer than eight inches) and pressure may be kept on the threads as the quillwork proceeds by placing the dowel under the feet or legs. It will be a little less handy than the preceding method, since the dowel may not spin off the correct amount of thread by

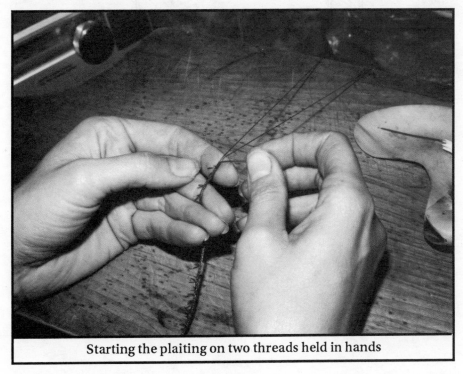

Starting the plaiting on two threads held in hands

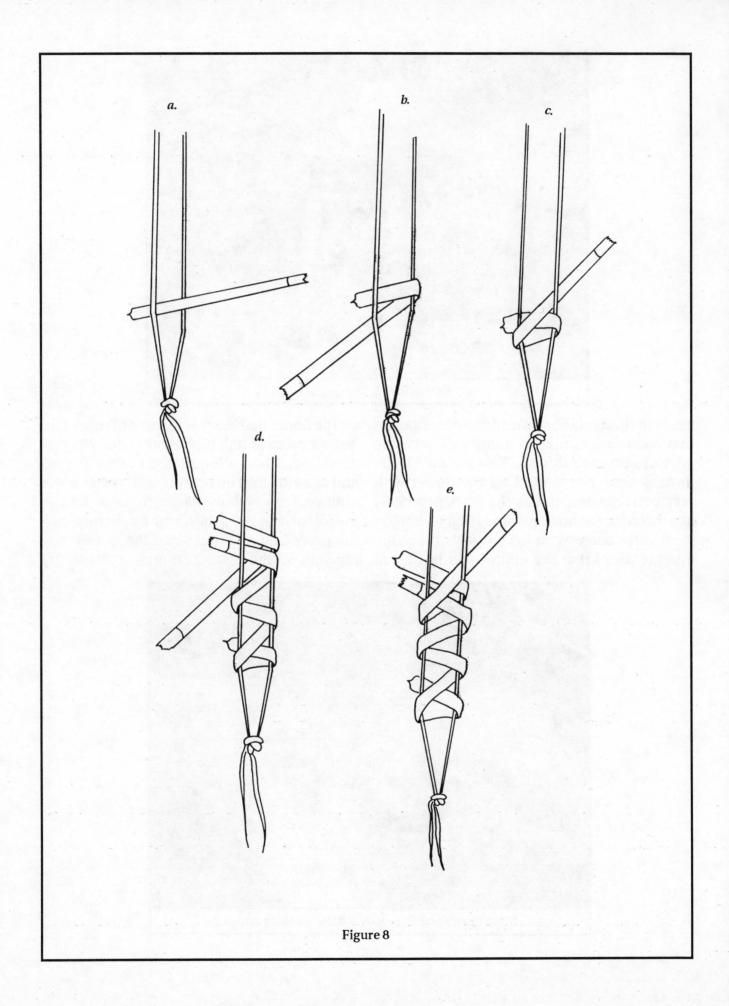

Figure 8

simply relieving the pressure of the feet or leg, and a hand may be needed to guide everything correctly. This method is an alternative to those who may not have a chair suited to the purposes of plaited quillwork.

The preferred thread for plaiting work is a Size F silk thread. The silk allows the quills to slide up and down easily which is a great help in compacting the folds of the quills. Sometimes it is also necessary to slide the folds around in accommodating color changes in the work. Heavy-weight cotton thread may be used as an alternative. Keep in mind that the size of the thread affects the coarseness or fineness of the plaited rows to some degree. Another factor, of course, is the size of the quills. The best plaited work is done with very fine, almost hair-like quills. The use of these quills necessitates the quilling of more rows on the piece and consequently few modern quillworkers bother to use them, which is a pity. A piece of plaited work made with finer quills is exceptionally beautiful, making the work well worth the effort. It is possible to pack the folds of fine quills very tightly and this completely hides the thread.

The technique used in plaiting is illustrated in **Figure 8**. Begin by casting an overhand knot in the threads. The knot will stabilize the threads by allowing an even tension to be placed on the threads as they are held in the hands at the start of the work (as shown in the Photograph at the bottom of Page 35). As the rows are wrapped around the object, this knot will have to be cut off to avoid having a lump under the quillwork; be sure to leave at least an inch between the knot and the start of the quillwork. Figures 8a, 8b and 8c show how to start the first quill. The end of the quill is laid under the thread on the left and over the thread on the right. The quill then folds over the right thread at such an angle that it comes out under the left thread and beneath its end. It then folds up over the left thread, crosses itself between the threads and is flipped under the right thread above the first fold on the right thread.

Continue plaiting the quill between the threads as shown in Figure 8d until there is only a small amount of color left on the quill. It

After several inches of plaiting are complete, the work is wound on the object to be quilled (in this case, a knife handle) and kept there until the work is completed.

37

is then necessary to splice in another quill. The splice must be started on the right side if the quillwork is wound on the piece from left to right. It must be made on the left side if the quillwork is wound on the piece from right to left. As these instructions wind from right to left (the easiest direction for right-handed quillworkers), the illustration shows the splice on the left. Lay the end of the new quill next to the tip of the old as shown in Figure 8d. It lies beneath the left thread and folds over the right thread so that it crosses beneath both quills and emerges under the left thread at such an angle that when it folds over the left thread it again crosses itself and the old tip. This time it crosses on the top. When the quillwork is compacted together, this will form an effective knot that will hold both ends in place. The quillwork continues (Figure 8e) with the new quill flipped under the right thread and ready to cross to the left once more.

After the work progresses a few inches, it may be wound on the piece to be decorated. Thereafter, the quillwork will be kept on the piece so that color changes and designs are placed in the work correctly. Even though the quills are not really soft at this point, the plaited quillwork will mold itself to the shape of the object quite rapidly and will retain that shape indefinitely.

The starting end of the quillwork is held down by folding the first inch or so under and winding succeeding rows over it as shown in the Photograph on Page 37. If there is a need to stop the work at any time after this point, simply wind four or five wraps of the thread around the object being quilled and tie the object to the dowel that holds the threads. The thread wraps should be fairly snug.

Continue to wind the rows of quillwork on the piece until they reach about an inch from the end of the work area. Then place a thread loop down and wind the rest of the rows over it. It will then be an easy matter to tuck the end of the quillwork under the preceding rows by placing the thread loop over the end of the quillwork and pulling it under itself. This is the same method that was used to finish the quill wrapping on Page 33, Figure 7h, except that this time you will be pulling the quilled row and not just one quill. There is no way to effectively flatten the quillwork after it has been wound on to the object. However, there should be no need to do so if small enough quills have been used and the quills have been flattened properly prior to being placed in the work.

Chapter IV
ADVANCED QUILLING TECHNIQUES

It is strongly suggested that the reader study the information in Chapters One through Three, understand how to use the techniques described therein and, if possible, master those methods before attempting the following techniques.

Two Quill Zigzag Technique

The Two Quill Zigzag technique is a simple yet striking quill technique. It is commonly found in border work and in quilled pictographs and lends a piece a fine and elaborate appearance which belies the actual simplicity of the technique.

As can be seen in **Figure 9**, the technique consists of the Zigzag Technique that is worked with two quills of different colors, one on top of the other. The backstitch is used and although Figure 9a illustrates the work beginning on the bottom guideline, it could be started on the top. Place the two quills on the leather, as shown in Figure 9a, and backstitch over them. Fold both quills up at the same time and stitch over them along the top guideline. Continue quilling in this manner until either of the quills is too short to completely cross the row twice.

The method of splicing is demonstrated in the remainder of Figure 9. To keep the splice from being too bulky, never splice both quills

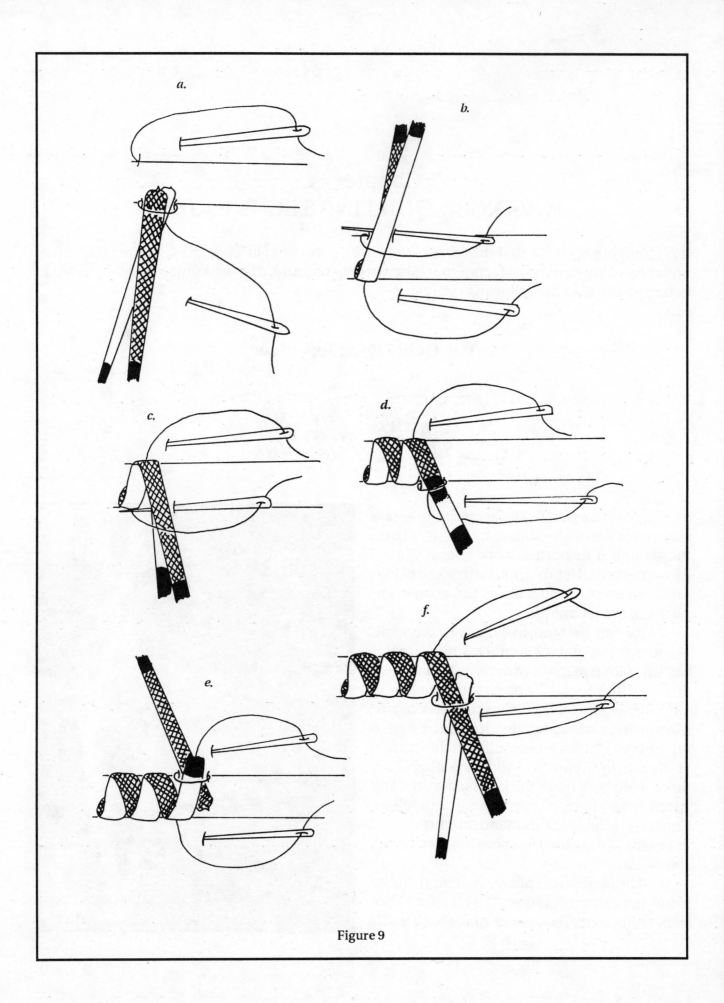

Figure 9

in the same stitch. Figure 9d shows the colored quill after it has been trimmed. As the colored quill shows only as the quills runs from the top of the row to the bottom, it is spliced in at the top of the row. It is easy to see that it has been cut off at the opposite side (bottom) of the row. The same method is used for the white quill. It is trimmed at the same stitch where the colored quill was spliced in as shown in Figure 9e.

The last illustration (Figure 9f) depicts the white quill being spliced in at the bottom of the row. This is necessary, as it shows when the quills run from the bottom of the row to the top. By trimming, folding and then splicing, the work is kept smooth with no bulky lumps. This technique is finished in the usual manner as shown in Figure 3 on Page 20.

Two Quill Triangle

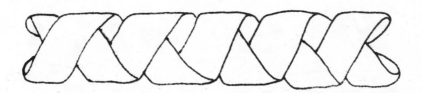

The Two Quill Triangle is another fairly simple multiple quill technique. Its use lends a piece an interesting texture and a lot of visual appeal. The early use of this technique prepares the quillworker for the more difficult manipulative skills required by some of the more complex multiple quill techniques.

Keep in mind, as the details in **Figure 10** are studied, that the quillwork is shown spread apart a good deal more than it actually should be so that it is easier to understand the technique. Two quills of the same color are used and they must be soft and wet enough so as not to stiffen as the work proceeds, but not so swelled with moisture that they will not flatten properly. Once again, the backstitch is used in this technique.

Stitch two flattened quills to the leather as shown in Figure 10a. Quill #1 is on the top guideline and Quill #2 on the bottom line. Next, the top quill (#1) is folded down and stitched to the bottom guideline as shown in Figure 10b. From this point on, each quill runs from the bottom line to the top and then back to the bottom again before the next quill is stitched in

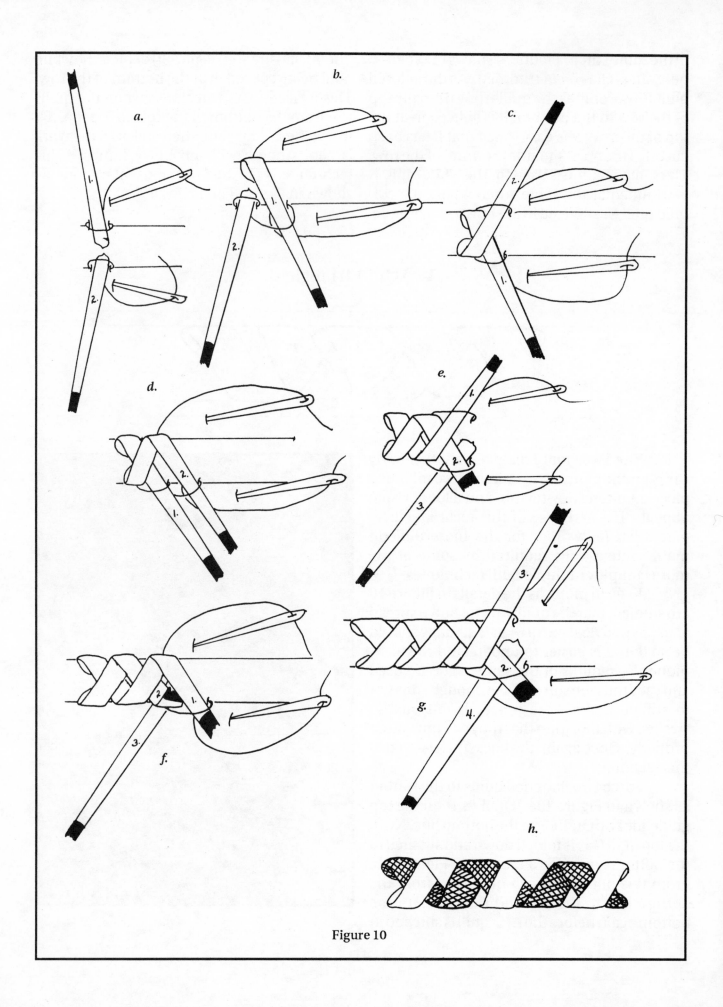

Figure 10

place. As can be seen, this technique is another modification of the zigzag technique.

Figure 10c and 10d shows Quill #2 stitched first to the top guideline and then to the bottom guideline. Figure 10e illustrates how a splice is made on Quill #2. As shown, Quill #1 has been stitched to the top guideline in the initial part of its circuit. This gets it out of the way for the moment and puts it in the proper position to cover the trimmed tip of Quill #2. Trim the tip of Quill #2 and loosen the stitch over it just a bit. Slide another flattened Quill (#3) under the stitch and pull it tight again. Figure 10f shows the trimmed tip of Quill #2 folded up and covered by Quill #1 as it continues on and is stitched to the bottom guideline. At this point Quill #1 will also need to be spliced and this is accomplished in the same manner; Figure 10g shows this splice. Once again, Quill #3 is stitched to the top guideline and Quill #2 is trimmed to the desired length and the stitch holding it is loosened so that flattened Quill #4 can be slid under it. The work continues as before: Quill #2 will be folded up and Quill #3 stitched over it. When the end of the row is reached, finish the quill in the normal manner as shown on page 20, Figure 3. It will look best if one quill is finished on the top guideline and one is finished on the bottom guideline.

A variation of the Two Quill Triangle, called the Two Quill Stripe, is illustrated in Figure 10h. This is worked in exactly the same way as the Two Quill Triangle except quills of two different colors are used. One color is started on the top guideline and the other color on the bottom. This variation makes a striking border on a piece and can also be used as an accent in a design.

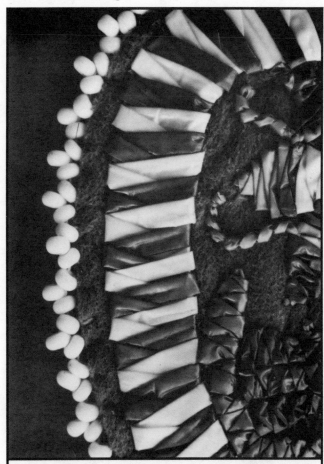

Two quill stripe variation of Two Quill Triangle

Two Quill Diamond

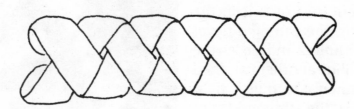

The Two Quill Diamond Technique is slightly more complex than the previous multiple quill methods. It is an adaptation of the simple band technique and employs two quills of the same color. This technique lends an interesting texture to rows of quillwork and can be worked in rows that are a bit wider than normal if that is desired. If extra wide rows are being quilled, try to use very long quills; normal length quills may be used otherwise.

Figure 11 demonstrates how the Two Quill Diamond is worked. Figure 11a shows two flattened quills backstitched to the leather; one on the top guideline and one on the bot-

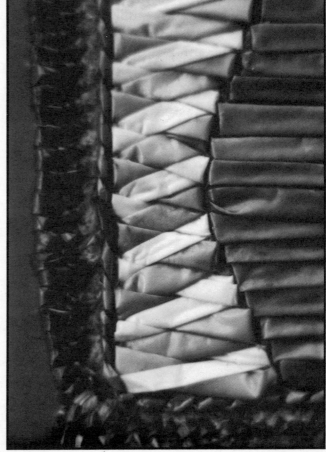

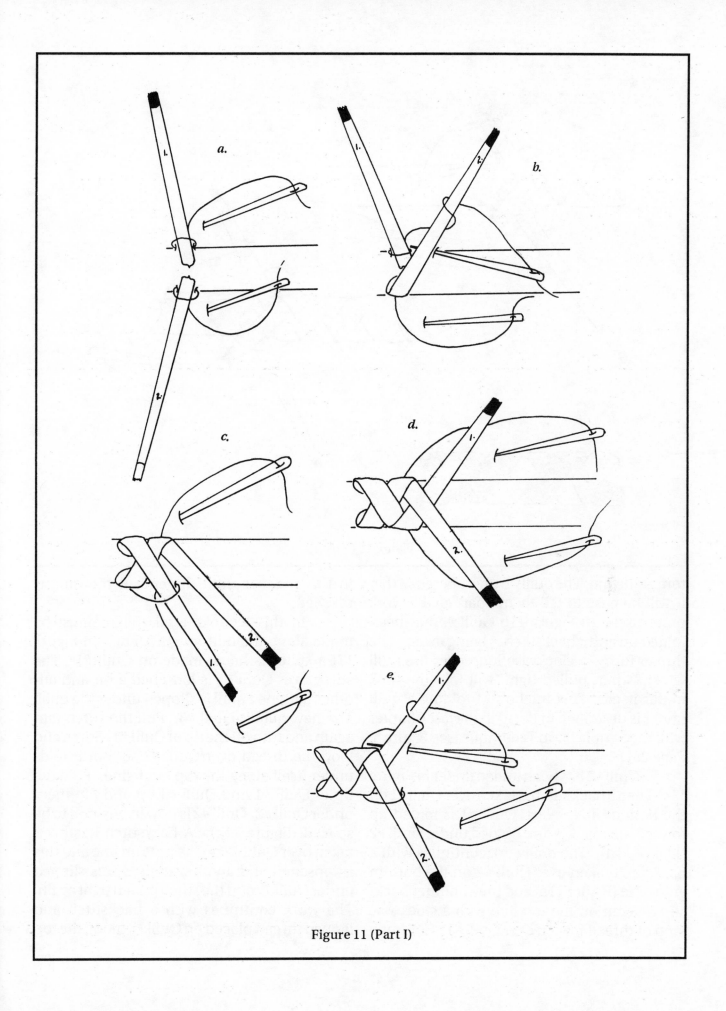

Figure 11 (Part I)

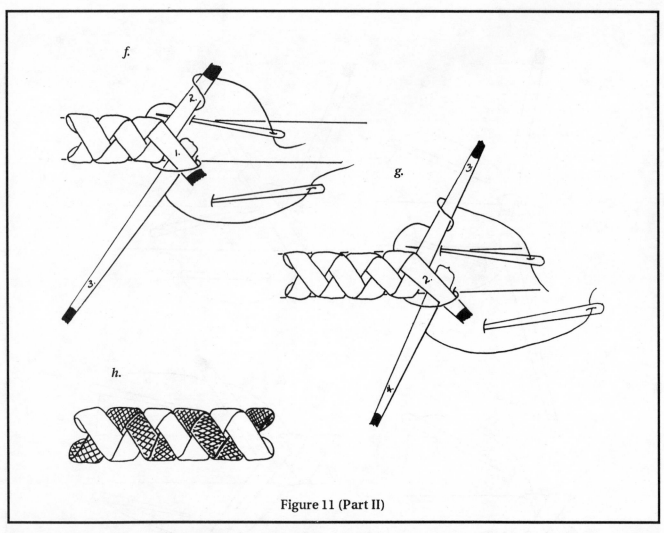

Figure 11 (Part II)

tom guideline. The quills are numbered so that it will be easy to tell them apart as the work progresses. In Figure 11b Quill #2 has been folded up and a backstitch is being taken. The thread forms a clockwise loop over the quill which, when pulled tight, will fold the quill under itself. This method of folding a quill under is described in detail in the last Chapter with the Simple Band Technique (see Figure 5, Page 26).

Quill #2 has been folded under in Figure 11c. Then a back stitch is taken over Quill #1 on the bottom line. Next, Quill #1 is folded up toward the top line and flipped under Quill #2 (Figure 11d). The quillwork continues with a backstitch taken over Quill #2 on the bottom guideline (Figure 11e) and then another backstitch taken on the top line with a clockwise loop of thread placed over Quill #1. Continue

in this manner until the end of the quill is reached.

In this technique all splices must be made along the bottom guideline. In Figure 11f a splice is being made on Quill #1. The stitch over Quill #1 is loosened a bit and another flattened quill is slipped under the quill. The new quill is Quill #3. Pull the stitch taut again and trim off the tip of Quill #1. Stitch and loop the thread over Quill #2 so that it folds under itself along the top guideline. Fold the tip of Quill #1 and Quill #3 up and flip them under Quill #2. Quill #2 is now in position to be spliced (Figure 11g). A backstitch has been taken over Quill #2 on the bottom line and this is loosened and another quill (#4) is slipped under Quill #2 and the stitch pulled tight again. The work continues with a backstitch and looped thread placed on Quill #3 along the top

46

PLATE I

PLATE II

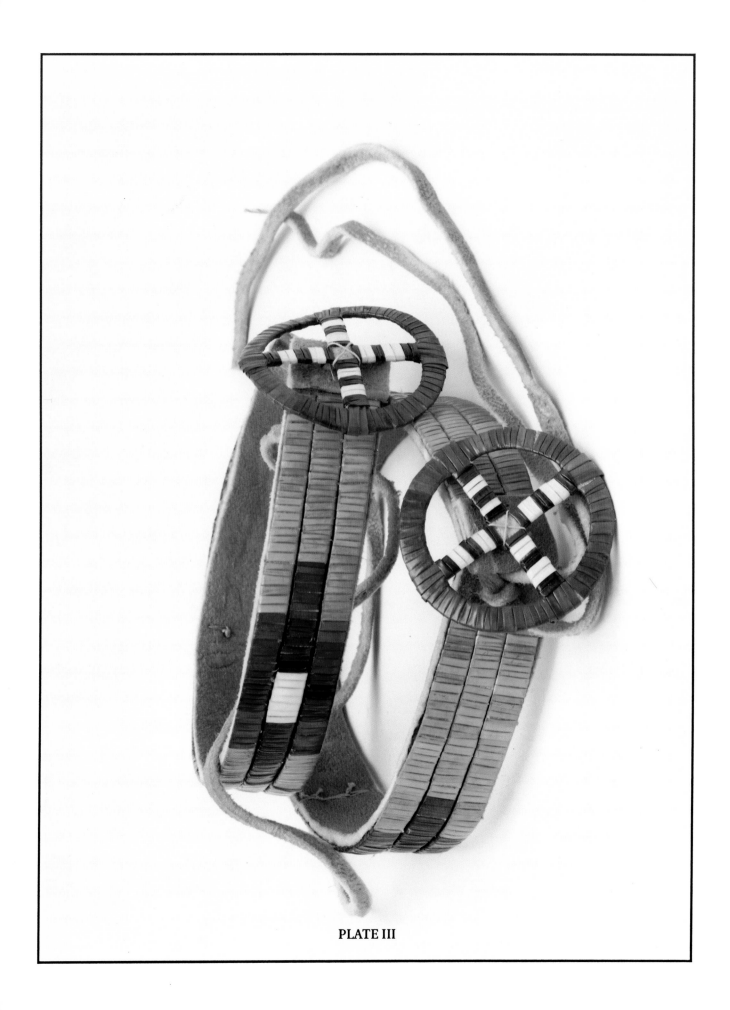

PLATE III

PLATE IV

line. Continue in this manner to the end of the row and then finish off the quills in the usual manner.

A variation of the Two Quill Diamond, called the Two Quill Diamond Stripe, is illustrated in Figure 11h. This technique is worked in exactly the same manner as the Two Quilled Diamond but two different colored quills are used. The color effect is the same as the Two Quill Stripe, shown in Figure 10, but there is a slight difference in the texture of this variation. This technique entails considerably more work in order to obtain the same color scheme. It will, however, work into decorative borders nicely.

Three Quill Double Diamond

This technique may be the most difficult one presented in this book. The Three Quill Double Diamond will require advanced manipulative skills and a great deal of patience. Basically it is an adaptation of the simple band technique but the looped back stitch is used along both the top and bottom guidelines and this presents the quillworker with difficult splicing. This technique is really only truly appreciated by those who have attempted it.

Figure 12a illustrates the correct starting position for the three quills. Note that Quill #1 is stitched to the leather in the middle of the row. It is best to keep it slightly above the exact center of the row. The quillwork begins by folding Quill #1 down as in Figure 12b and taking a backstitch on the bottom guideline. A loop of thread is placed over the quill in a counter-clockwise direction so that when the backstitch is pulled tight the quill will fold under itself and end by pointing upwards (Figure 12c). Also illustrated in Figure 12c, Quill #2 has been folded up over Quill #1 and is being stitched down with another looped backstitch. This time the thread loop runs clockwise. Remember that along the top guideline the loop is always clockwise and that along the bottom guideline the loop is always made

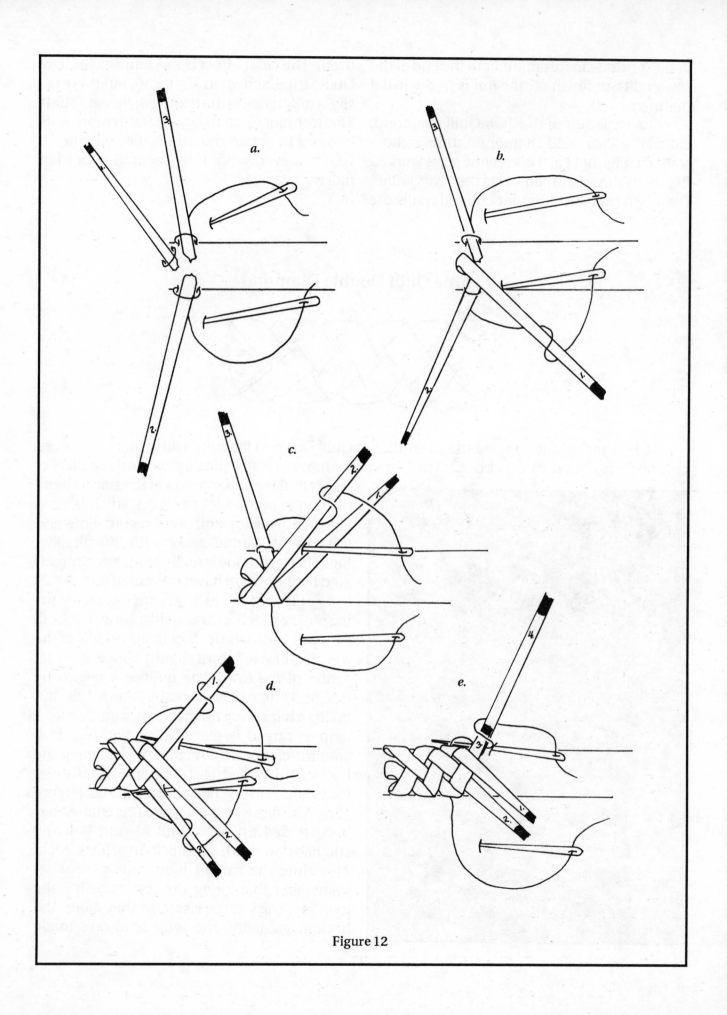

Figure 12

counter-clockwise.

The last quill may now be folded down and plaited into the work. Quill #3 folds down over the first length of Quill #2 and is flipped under the second length of Quill #1. If that sounds a bit confusing, study Figure 12d. In this case, one picture is worth a million words. As soon as Quill #3 is plaited into the work, it is also stitched down to the bottom guideline and folded under itself so that it will be pointed toward the top line. The work progresses in this manner until the end of the quill is reached.

A new quill is shown being spliced in behind Quill #3 in Figure 12e. Note that in this instance the new quill must be in place before the stitch can be taken. This is a departure from most of the splices discussed up to this time when it has been possible to simply loosen the stitch and slip the new quill under the existing stitch and old quill. Keeping the two quills neat and orderly as the stitch pulls tight and folds them under is a little bit of a trick but can be accomplished with some practice. Each of the quills may be trimmed to the usual half-row length and spliced in this manner.

The illustration shows the splice always made along the top guideline and though this is preferable, it is not a rule and splices may be made any place where convenient in actual practice. Continue quilling to the end of the row and then finish off the ends of the three quills in the manner previously explained. The proper position of the finished quills can be seen illustrated in the figure at the beginning of this section.

Multiple Quill Plait

Another technique that requires advanced manipulative skills is the Multiple Quill Plait. It is a good technique to master and is not as difficult as it looks. Pieces worked with this technique are always impressive and the work moves along at a fairly rapid pace making it an all time favorite with quillworkers who take the time to learn the skill.

Multiple Quill Plait can be worked in extra wide rows. The only limit to row width is determined by the length of the quills and, as the technique is presented in this section, the quill must be capable of reaching across the row twice. With careful quill selection it is possible to have rows as wide as 1 1/4 inch. Of course the rows may also be worked narrower. If a narrow row is desired, the number of quills in the plait may have to be reduced. The back-stitch and looped backstitch are used in this technique.

A favorite form of the Multiple Quill Plait is worked with six (6) quills as presented in

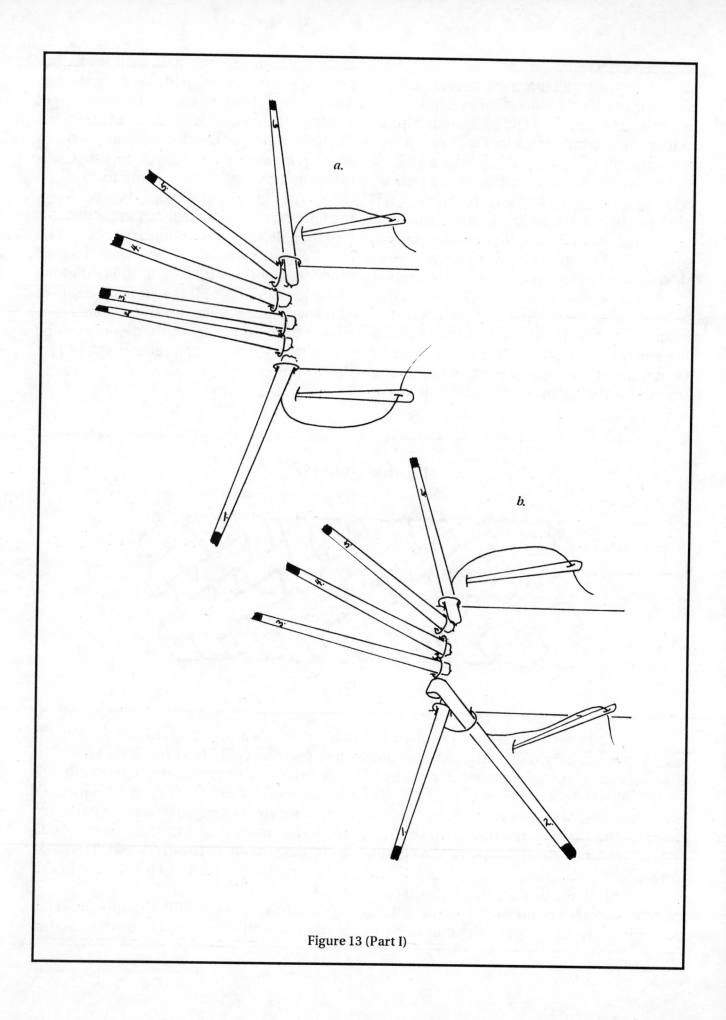

a.

b.

Figure 13 (Part I)

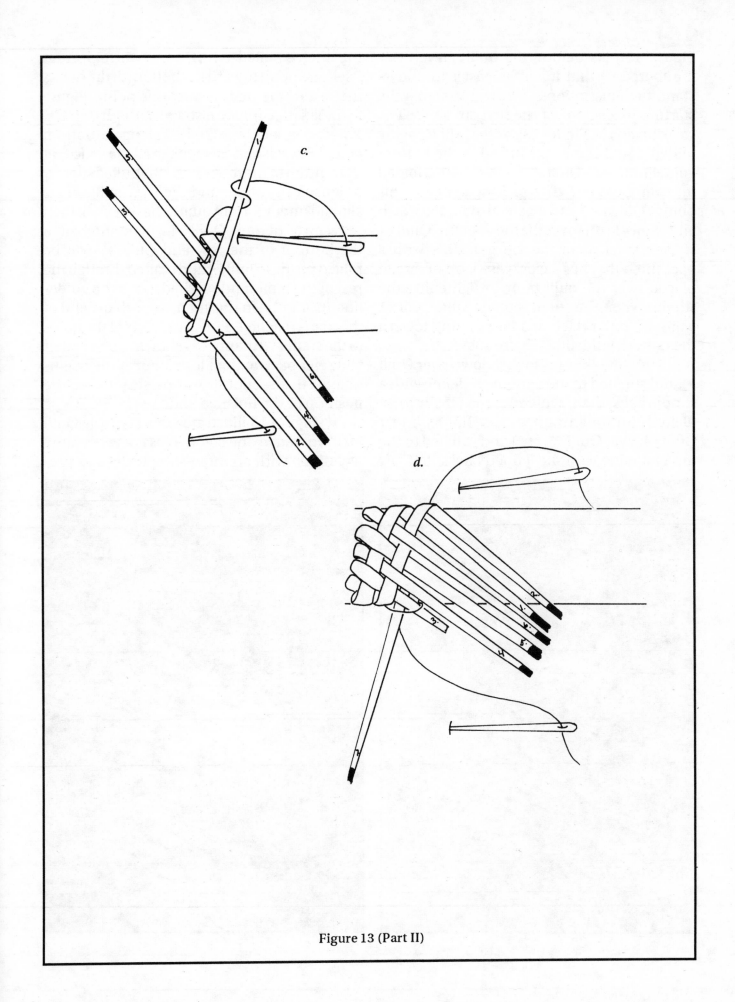

Figure 13 (Part II)

Figure 13. As before, the quills have been numbered so that it will be easier to understand the illustrations. Figure 13a shows the starting placement of the first six quills. The work begins in Figure 13b with Quill #2 being folded down and backstitched to the bottom guideline beside Quill #1. Quill #1 is then folded up over Quill #2. The plaiting starts at this point. Quills #4 and #6 are also folded down and Quill #1 runs over the top of them. Quill #1 is then stitched to the top guideline with a backstitch that has a clockwise loop of thread placed over the quill prior to tightening the stitch. When the stitch is made taut, Quill #1 will fold under itself and be pointing toward the bottom guideline (Figure 13c).

Now Quill #3 is folded down over Quill #1 and stitched to the bottom guideline with a simple backstitch. Quill #2 is then ready to be plaited up through the row (over Quill #3, under Quill #4, over Quill #5, etc.) and stitched to the top guideline with the looped backstitch. As the stitch is pulled tight, Quill #2 will fold under itself and point toward the bottom of the row as the rest of the quills are at this point (Figure 13d). This illustration also shows the first splice. This takes place with Quill #3 along the bottom guideline. It is easiest to make all the splices at the bottom of the row. Quill #3 is pulled slightly to loosen the stitch and the next quill (#7) is slipped under the old quill. The work will then proceed as before. Quill #4 will be stitched to the bottom of the row and Quill #7 will be folded up over Quill #4 and plaited through the rest of the quills and stitched to the top guideline. Continue in this manner until the end of the row is reached. Finish the ends of the quills in the standard manner as shown in Figure 3. If you refer back to the illustration at the beginning of this section it will be easy to see the position of the finished ends.

Figure 13 illustrates this Multiple Quill Plait worked in one color. This is a very sturdy technique with an interesting texture as pre-

sented, but it is possible to add intricate color schemes as well. The photograph on the bottom right of Page 52 is a piece worked in a color scheme called Multiple Quill Plait. There are many possibilities with this technique and the quillworker should do a lot of experimenting with it.

Checker Weave

The Checker Weave Technique is most often used to cover large areas with quillwork such as legging strips, knife sheaths, etc. It is usually worked with quills of one color, but a geometric pattern may be made by using quills of different colors. This technique has been ignored for the most part in modern quillwork as so few quillworkers understand the simple procedure that is presented in this book for getting a quill to fold under itself. A vast majority who have attempted the technique manually fold the quills over a needle and stitch them down in one manner or another. This takes an enormous amount of time and prevents the quillworker from making full use of the capabilities inherent in the craft. So, if you have not mastered the looped backstitch, be sure to go back over the Simple Band Technique until those skills are understood.

The Checker Weave Technique is a complex form of the Simple Band Technique and all of the rules that applied there are to be

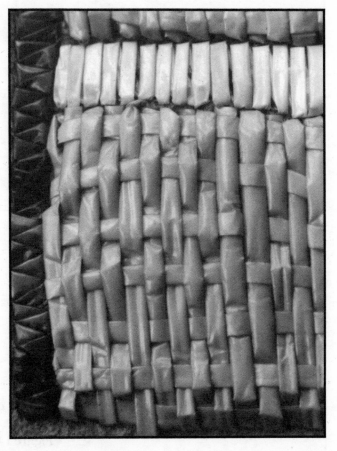

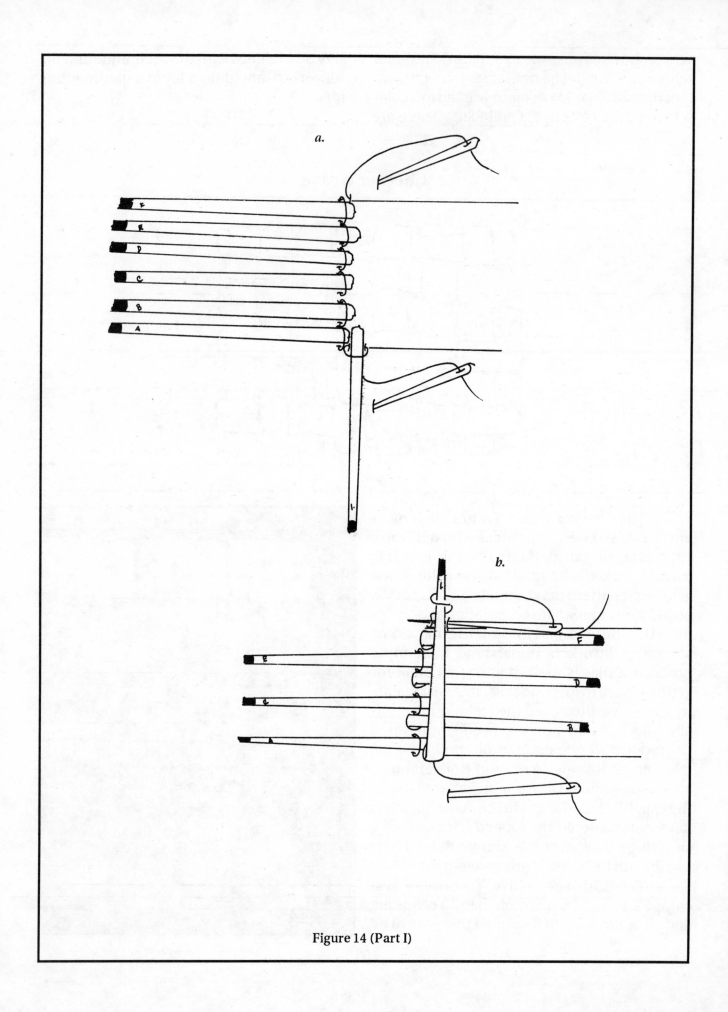

Figure 14 (Part I)

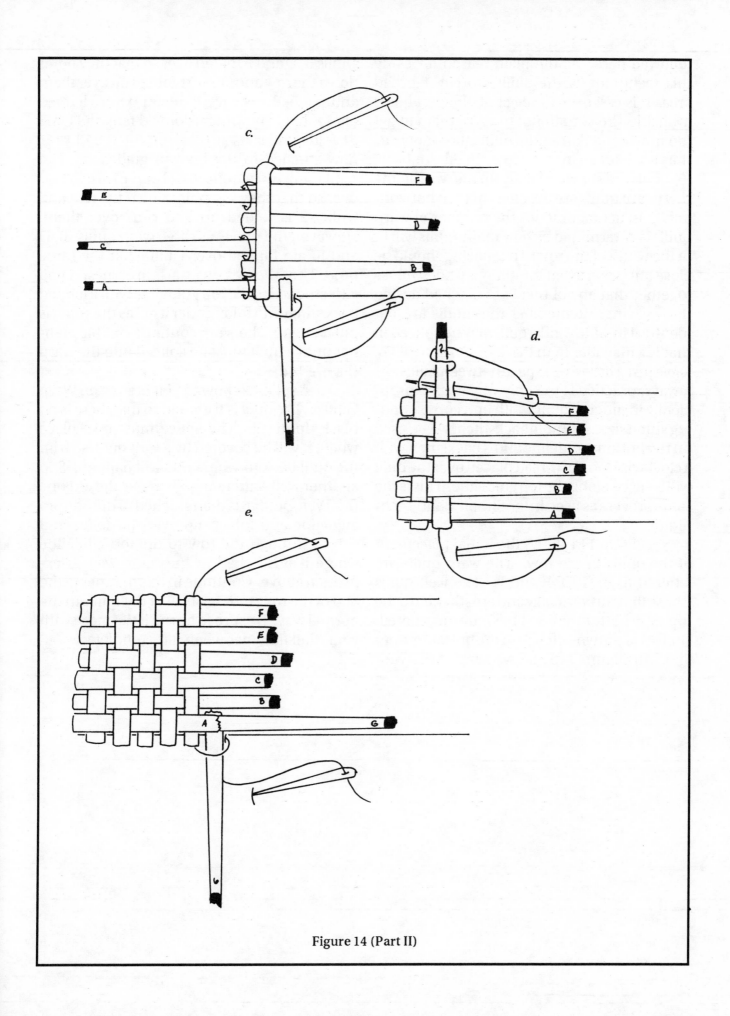

Figure 14 (Part II)

followed here. As the main reason for using this technique is the ability to cover broad areas it is essential to select the longest quills available. Be certain not to allow them to get too moist and flatten the quills thoroughly as they are worked into the row. In **Figure 14** six (6) quills are shown making up the warp in the row (warp quills are the ones that run horizontally). In actual practice the number of warp quills is determined by how many quills will fit in the width of the row. The spacing should be close but be sure that the quills are not so close together that any of them are pinched during the weaving. Remember that quills are not identical in width and a quill may be spliced in that is a bit wider than the last; for this reason, leave just a little extra space between quills. As always, practice is the only way to gain proficiency in judging quill width and corresponding stitch size. A simple backstitch will be used on the bottom guideline and a backstitch with a clockwise loop of thread placed over the quill will be used along the top guideline. This is the same process as used in the Simple Band Technique.

Figure 14a shows the initial placement of the quills in the row. The warp quills are lettered A, B, C, D, E and F. The weft quills (those that run vertically and are stitched to the top and bottom guide lines) are numbered. Quill #1 is shown stitched to the bottom guideline. In Figure 14b the weaving starts with Quills B, D and F folded over so that they point down the row and Quill #1 folded up over them and stitched at the top guideline with a looped backstitch. The stitch is pulled taut and Quill #1 folds under itself (Figure 14c). Quill #2 is now stitched to the bottom guideline. The remaining warp quills (A, C and E) are folded over so that they too point down the row and Quill #2 is folded up and runs over them. However, the previous three warp quills (B, D and F) are flipped over Quill #2 at the same time. Thus the weaving starts in earnest. Quill #2 is stitched to the top guideline with a looped back stitch and folds under itself as the stitch is pulled tight. The work continues in this manner until a quill must be spliced into the warp (Figure 14d).

A splice is shown in Figure 14e on Warp Quill A. The quill is trimmed so that there is no black tip at all. The splice must take place where it will be covered by a weft quill, so trim the quill back to where this will happen. Slip another well flattened quill under the old one (A). Weft Quill #6 is then stitched to the bottom guideline and folded up over the splice and woven through the row to the top guideline where it is stitched in the same way as explained above. Continue in this manner to the end of the row and finish all of the quills in the normal way. Be sure to burnish the piece with your quill flattener when it is complete.

Single Thread Sawtooth Technique

The Single Thread Sawtooth Technique is well suited to floral quillwork and to the curvilinear designs found in some eastern- and midwestern-styles of quillwork. This technique gives a piece a great deal of visual appeal that makes up for the fact that it is not as strong as some other types of quillwork. It has a tendency to snag and is prone to tear out more easily than other forms of quilling. If this is kept in mind, and the use of the Single Thread Sawtooth is relegated to pieces which will receive a minimum of abuse, it is an exciting technique to use.

In this technique the horizontal spot stitch will be used (refer to Figure 2b on Page 19). Because of the change in stitch from what has been used before, the manipulation of the leather, quills and needle will be entirely different. It will be useful to spend a little time practicing the Single Thread Sawtooth on a scrap of leather before starting an actual piece of quillwork. Use moderation in selecting the quill size. A thick quill is very difficult to work in this technique but using too small a quill will prevent clean, even folds which are necessary in forming the small "teeth" on either side of the guideline. For this technique, flatten the quills thoroughly.

Figure 15a shows the starting position of the first quill. It has been stitched to the leather with a back stitch but all further work is done with the horizontal spot stitch. After securing the quill to the leather the first spot stitch is taken to the right of the quill. When the stitch is pulled tight the thread will have crossed over the quill a second time (Figure 15b). Begin the first sawtooth by folding the quill to the

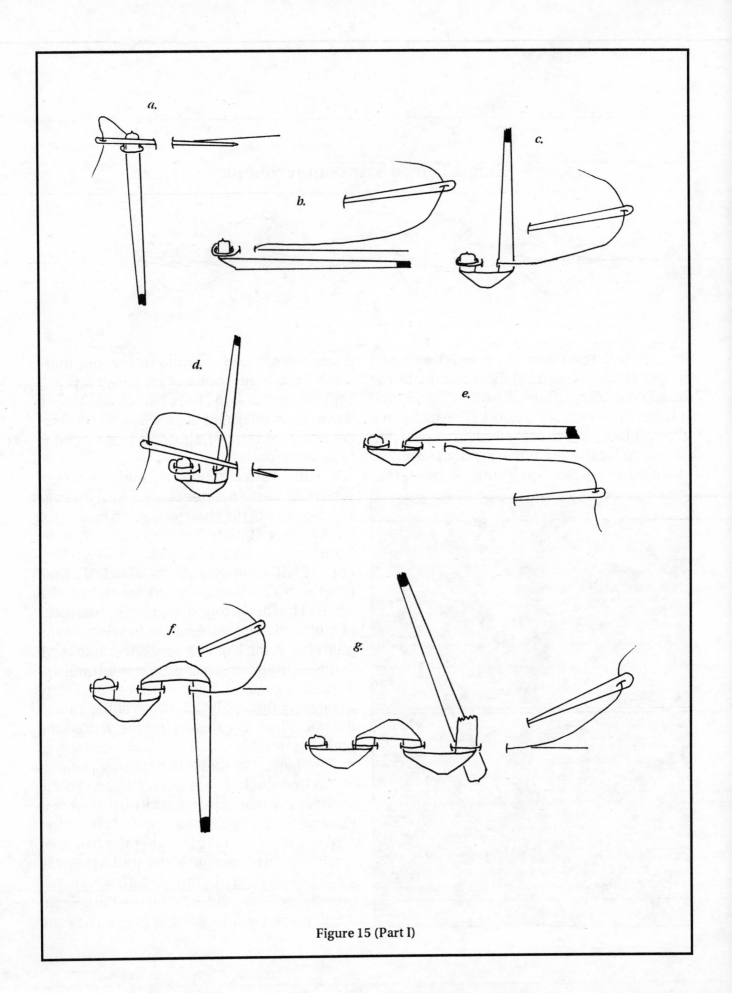

Figure 15 (Part I)

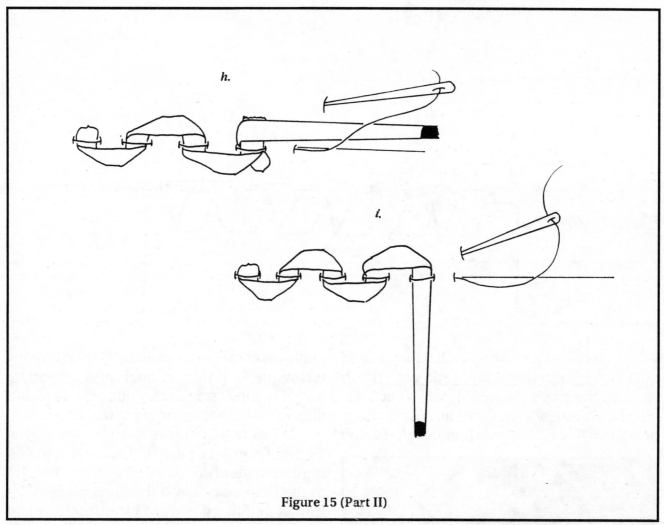

Figure 15 (Part II)

right, parallel to the guideline. Complete the first sawtooth by holding the thread firmly and folding the quill up and around the thread as shown in Figure 15c. Hold the quill in place and take another small spot stitch over the quill (Figure 15d). The second sawtooth is formed as the quill is again folded parallel to the guideline (Figure 15e) and then wrapped around the thread so that it now points down as in Figure 15f. Continue in this way until the end of the quill is reached. A second quill is shown being spliced into the row in Figure 15g, 15h and 15i. Trim the end of the old quill and loosen the last stitch holding it down. Flatten a new quill and slip it under the old one. Pull the stitch tight again and fold the new quill around the old tip to the right so that it is parallel to the guideline. Proceed as before until the end of the row is reached. Finish the row of quillwork by stitching over the last fold in the quill several times; this is shown in the Figure at the beginning of this section. Be sure to flatten the row once again when you are finished. The flatter this technique is made, the less likely that it will snag and rip out.

Zigzag Edging Technique

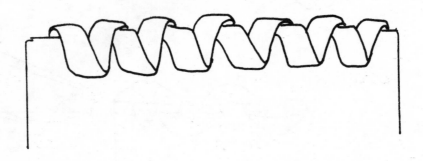

To create a finished look on a piece of quillwork it is often desirable to do some finish work on the edges. Sometimes this is accomplished with beads, but a quilled edge really presents a fine look and an opportunity for the quillworker to show off a little. This first edging technique is simple enough and is really a repeat of the Zigzag Technique explained and illustrated in the beginning of this book.

Figure 16a shows the way the Zigzag Edging Technique begins. The work starts on the underside of the leather which is referred to as the flesh side. Lay a flattened quill on the leather pointing down away from the edge and stitch over it by poking the needle all the way through the leather. Pull the stitch tight and then fold the quill over the edge of the leather so that it is lying on the top or grain side of the leather (Figure 16b). The illustration in Figure 16c is from the grain side of the hide and shows another stitch taken over the quill. The needle, once again, has been taken all the way through the leather. The stitch is pulled tight and the quill is folded back to the flesh side of the leather (Figure 16d). Even though the technique is illustrated from both sides of the leather, in actual practice it is seldom necessary to turn the leather over as the work progresses. Doing so slows the work and the practice should be avoided when possible. Work with the grain side of the leather facing you so it is possible to watch this side (the side showing on the finished piece) and keep the work on

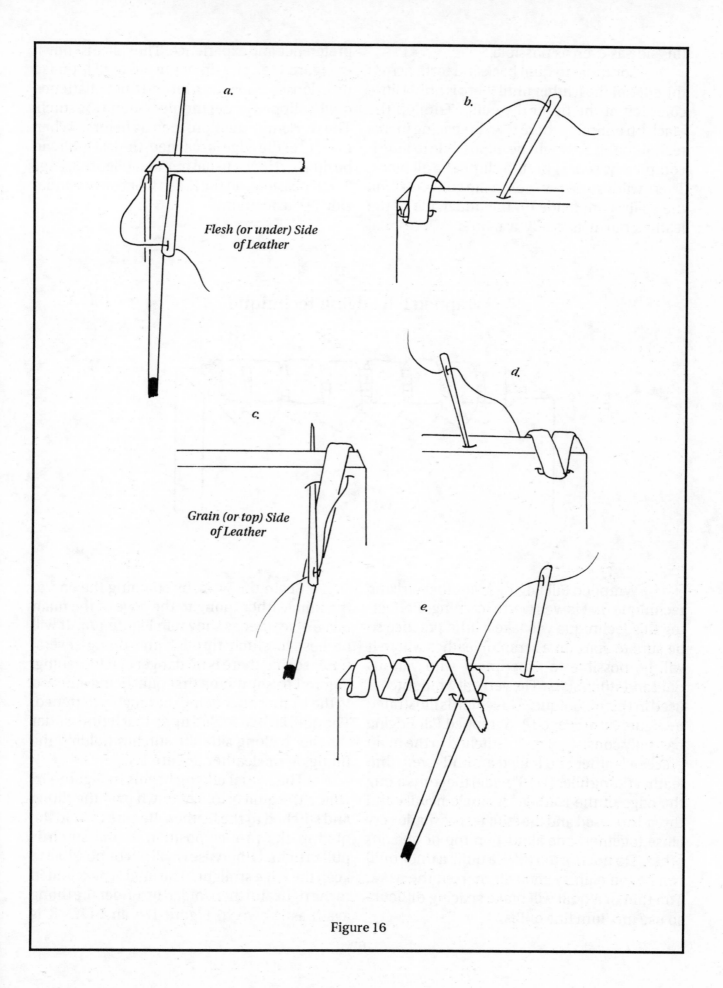

a.

Flesh (or under) Side of Leather

b.

c.

Grain (or top) Side of Leather

d.

e.

Figure 16

this side as even as possible.

Continue to quill back and forth across the edge of the leather until there is only a little color left at the tip of the quill. Trim off the black tip entirely - there is wide spacing in this technique and it might be impossible to hide it completely, so it is best to eliminate all black. There will be a neater look to the quillwork if all the splices are made on the underside of the leather but it is really a matter of personal preference and experience. The splice is shown in Figure 16e. The tip of the old quill is pulled up to loosen the stitch a bit and a new, flattened quill is slipped under the old one and the stitch. The work may then proceed as before. When the end of the edge is reached, the last quill can be finished in the usual manner (Figure 3, Page 20). If possible, do the finish work on the under side of the leather.

Wrapped Fill Edging Technique

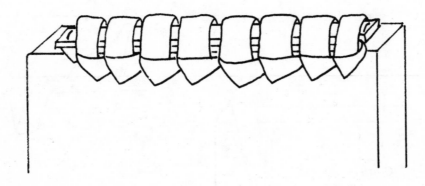

Wrapped Fill Edging is another striking technique that is well worth learning. Perfecting this technique will take a little practice so be sure to start on a scrap of leather where it will be possible to experiment with various quill and stitch sizes. The vertical whip stitch is used in this technique. This stitch is illustrated in Figure 2c on Page 19. Wrapped Fill Edging basically consists of quills stitched to the main piece of leather and folded around a very thin leather thong filler (1/16" wide) that runs along the edge of the leather. A single needle and thread are used and the stitches are made very close together, one almost on top of one another. Do not use too thick a quill; a thick quill will be too clumsy and will coarsen the work. Too thin of a quill will make spacing difficult, so use medium fine quills.

Begin the work by stitching the end of the thin leather thong to the edge of the main piece of leather as shown in Figure 17a. It will be best to stitch through the thong several times so that there is no danger of it loosening. Figure 17b shows the first quill being stitched to the leather after being thoroughly flattened. The quill is then folded up so that it runs under the thong along side the stitches holding the thong on the leather (Figure 17c).

The actual edging begins in Figure 17d where the quill is folded down over the thong and stitched to the leather. Be sure to hold the quill in the proper position as the stitch is pulled tight. Otherwise it will not be possible to keep the edge straight. The quill is next folded to the right and then folded up under the thong again as shown in Figure 17e and 17f. It is

62

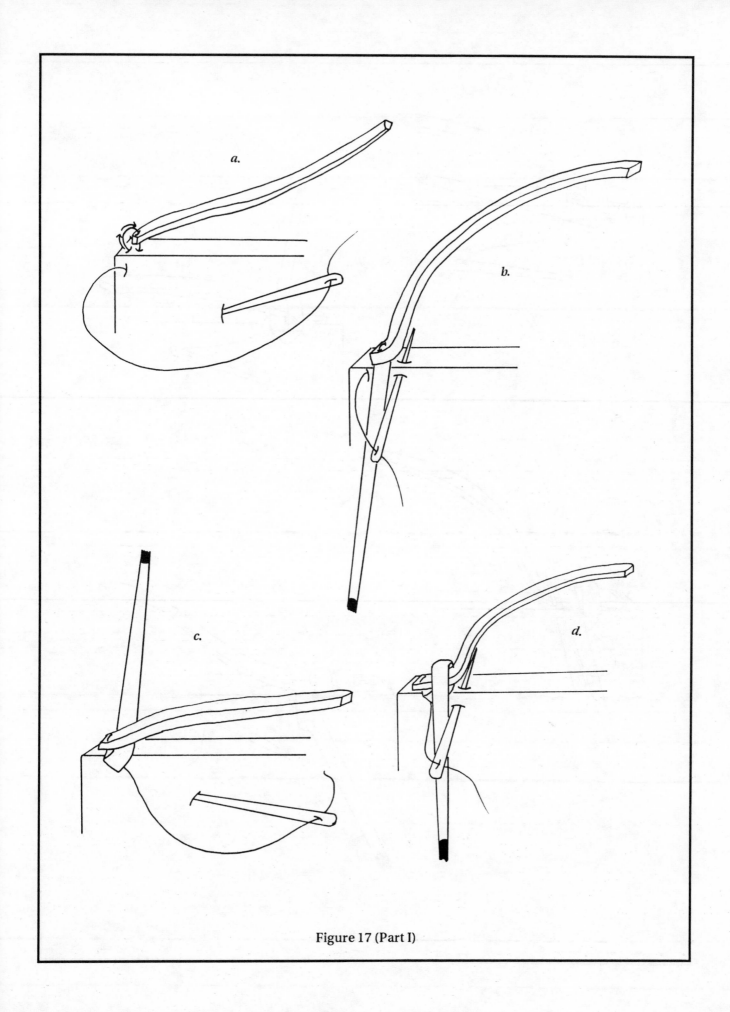

Figure 17 (Part I)

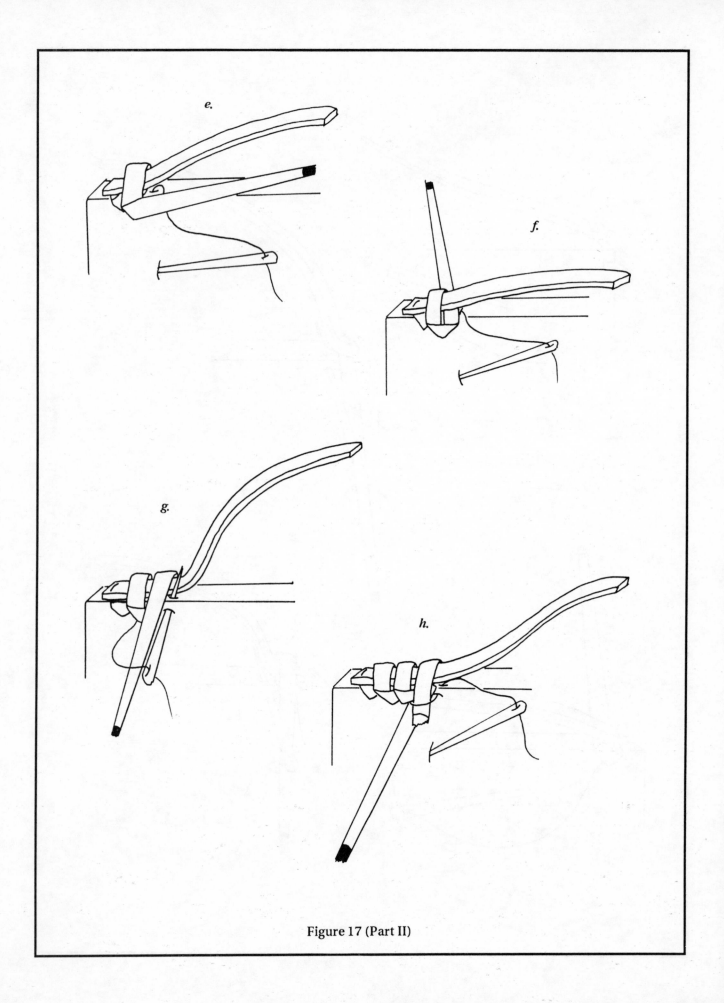

Figure 17 (Part II)

important to hold the thread firmly as the folds are made. The quill will tend to loosen the stitch as the folds are made if the thread is not held in place. In Figure 17g the quill has once again been folded down over the thong and stitched to the main leather piece. Continue to quill in the same manner until the end of the quill is reached. Figure 17h illustrates how to splice a new quill into the work. It is the same method that is used in many of the other techniques in this book. Loosen the last stitch a little by pulling up on the end of the old quill. Slip the new quill under the old and pull the stitch tight again. It is not necessary to trim the end of the old quill at this time. The new quill will then be folded to the right and wrapped around the leather thong, as was the previous quill, and stitched to the leather.

Continue in this way until the end of the edge is reached. Finish the last quill by stitching over it twice and trimming off the end. Then stitch the other end of the thong to the leather with two more stitches and knot the thread with three small stitches taken on the back side of the piece. This knot has been used to finish all of the projects and is illustrated in Figure 3 on Page 20. Trim off the excess length of thong and then trim all the quill ends sticking out of the back of the piece as close to the rest of the quillwork as possible.

Coiled Wrapping Technique

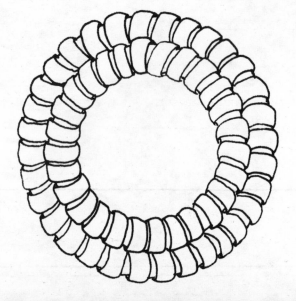

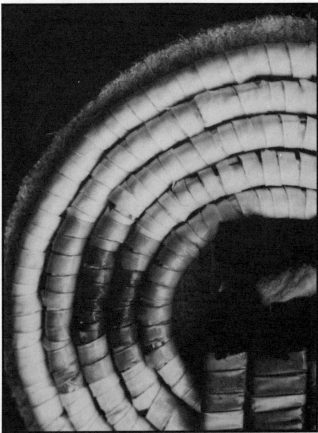

A three dimensional effect may be created on rosettes and strips with the Coiled Wrapping Technique. It is an adaptation of quill wrapping as described on Page 32, Figure 7. It is a good idea to study Figure 7 if this has not already been done. Sewing the quill wrapping to the leather complicates the technique tremendously and advanced manipulative skills are required to master this technique.

In older pieces worked in this technique a filler of horse hair was used. This is a very good medium to work on but most modern quillworkers prefer to use a very fine sash cord (approximately 1/8" in diameter) found at most hardware stores. It eliminates the splices that must be made in a horse hair filler. A medium width quill is most desirable for this technique and the longer the quill, the better. Try to use quills that will wrap around the cord at least three times. This will allow the quillwork to be stitched down every second or third wrap.

Begin the piece by carefully drawing a circle on the leather of the size required for the finished rosette. This is the only guideline that will be used. The beginning quillworker may find it helpful to draw the complete rosette design on a piece of paper and follow the plan as the coils are stitched to the leather. Figure 18a illustrates how the first quill is laid on the filler and Figure 18b shows how the wrapping starts. All of this should be familiar to the craftsperson who has mastered wrapping techniques presented earlier in this book. Figure 18c depicts the wrapped filler being stitched to the leather along the guideline. A simple spot stitch is used in the Coiled Wrapping Technique. In the illustration the thread emerges

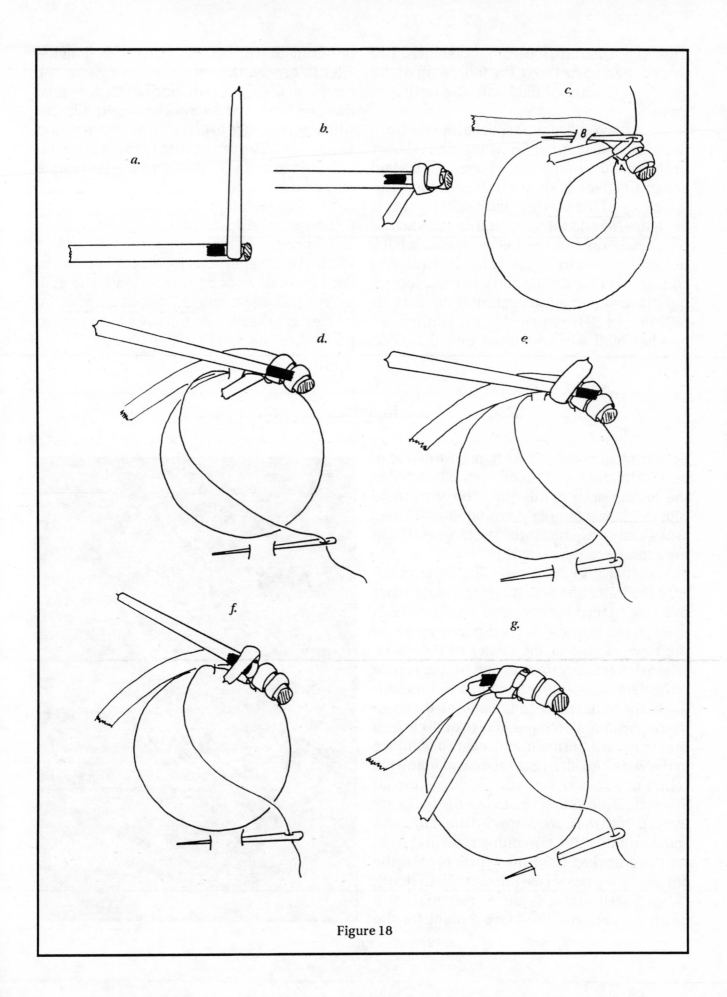

Figure 18

from a knot made in the leather at Point A. The thread then passes over the follicle tip of the quill and is stitched back into the leather at Point B.

A new quill may be spliced into the work in the normal manner for wrapping as shown in Figure 18d through 18g. A second quill is laid across the filler as shown in Figure 18d. The follicle tip of the previous quill folds up over it in Figure 18e and then the quill tip folds across the follicle tip and the follicle tip folds back down as shown in Figure 18f. The wrapping continues in Figure 18g and when the second quill is wrapped entirely around the filler its follicle tip will be stitched to the leather and another quill will be spliced into the work.

Continue to work in this manner, coiling the filler in toward the center of the rosette. Be careful to keep the work pushed back against the previous row as succeeding quills are stitched into place to keep the rosette as round as possible. The very center of the rosette can be left open or the Single Quill Line Technique may be used as fill.

This technique may also be employed for the quilled strips sometimes found on shirts and leggings. In these cases, the filler will be stitched in straight rows instead of in coils. In both types of work be sure to place the quill splices well down on the filler, as close to the leather as possible. As the rows form next to each other, the splices will be hidden.

Rosettes

For the most part, rosettes make use of one of four techniques. Filled coil work is covered in the section prior to this one. The other techniques - Zigzag, Simple Band and Single Thread Line - were presented in the last chapter. Quilling a rosette requires some proficiency in quill spacing because the outer guideline is longer than the inner one and, therefore, the stitches must be spaced farther apart on the outside than on the inside. This is especially true for the rows closest to the center of the circle. When first quilling rosettes, it is best to leave a rather large opening in the center. As the quillworker becomes more confident with the spacing requirements, it is possible to quill close to the center and still maintain a neat appearance in the work. An alternate method of filling the center of a rosette is to use the single thread line technique. In this instance, the quills are worked from the outside toward the center in a spiral and then the remaining rows in the rosette are worked from the center toward the outside of the piece (see Photograph to right).

A well drawn layout is essential for a neatly quilled rosette. Mark a point for the

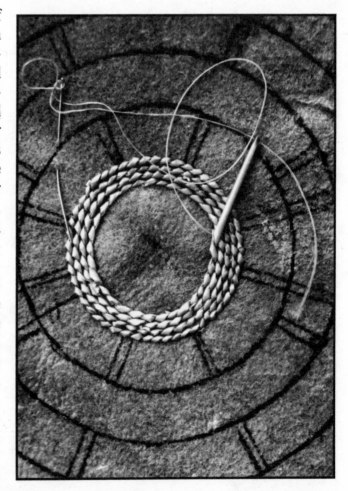

68

center of the rosette with a very fine tipped marking pen, and place the point of a compass on the mark each time a row is drawn on the leather. If the compass uses a pencil, be sure to carefully trace over the lines with a marking pen. It is very important to maintain a true circle as the tracing progresses. The center point is also used as a reference point when drawing the designs into the rows of the rosette. Lines that should be exactly opposite to each other in the rosette can be accurately drawn by spanning the circle with a ruler, the edge of which always crosses the center point.

The one other essential for a neatly quilled rosette is quills of similar width. This is especially important if the rosette is quilled with the simple band technique. The quills must also be flattened well. Take care that they are not too moist at any time during the work as this will prevent a good initial flattening and the final burnishing will not make up for an incomplete initial flattening.

When first starting to quill rosettes, one should use the technique that is most comfortable and the one with which the quillworker is most familiar. This will make the spacing variation easier to adjust too. In most instances, the beginner should start with the Zigzag Technique (Figure 19a) presented at the beginning of this book (Pgs 22-24). The work begins on the innermost row and the first quill should be

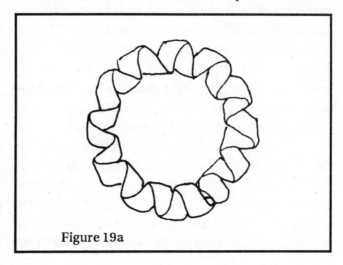

Figure 19a

69

stitched to the outer guideline at the start. If the quills seem to slant one way or the other as the work continues around the circle, simply extend or shorten the spacing between the stitches required. If the problem does not resolve itself in just a couple of stitches, the quill-worker must be ready to tear out the slanted quills back to a point where the work is acceptable. In no time at all, it will become second nature to make the proper spacing adjustments as the work proceeds. When the inner row is completed, continue to work by moving to the next row out from the center. The quillwork continues in this manner until the rosette is finished.

The Simple Band technique (Figure 19b)

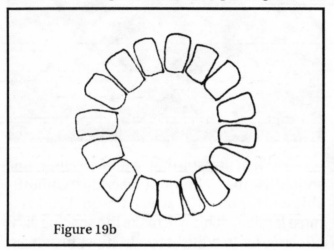

Figure 19b

makes the most geometrically uniform rosettes possible; it truly presents the quilled rosette in its very best form. When it is well executed, it approaches perfection in the mastering of the quilled art form and, as such, it is an achievement for which it is worth striving. Before attempting a rosette in the Simple Band Technique, be sure that there is a complete understanding of the technique in its straight row form (Pgs 25-27). Then, it should not be too difficult to transfer to the round version.

The rosette is worked in the same manner as the Zigzag Technique (Pgs 22-24), starting with the inner most row. Take the initial stitch over the first quill on the outer guideline of the row. Quill around the row as slowly as needed at first. This inner row will be the most

difficult one in the rosette. The circle is tighter than the following ones and it requires wider spacing along the outer guideline and closer spacing along the inner guideline than will the following rows. Again, watch for any slant developing in the quills as they reach across the

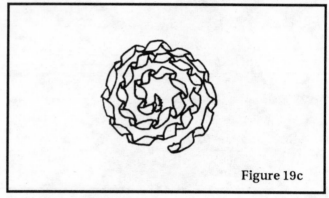

Figure 19c

row. This indicates that the spacing is not correct. If it is caught in time, it will be an easy matter to adjust the spacing with longer or shorter stitches.

Single Thread Line technique (Pgs 28-30 & Figure 19c) is often used to fill the center

70

of a rosette that is otherwise quilled with another technique, but it may also be used effectively alone to fill an entire rosette. With this technique, the work will start along the outside guideline. In many instances, the outer guideline is the only one drawn when using this technique, but at times it is helpful to have also marked some of the color changes so that these will always be placed correctly. The quillwork spirals from the outer edge toward the center of the rosette as the work proceeds. It is very nearly impossible to keep this technique absolutely round as the spiral form, so quite often its use is limited to rosettes of smaller diameter or to rosettes with few, if any, vertical and diagonal color changes.

The fourth common technique employed in the making of rosettes is Filled Coil Wrapping (Figure 19d). This has been covered in the section above (Pgs 66-68) and the reader

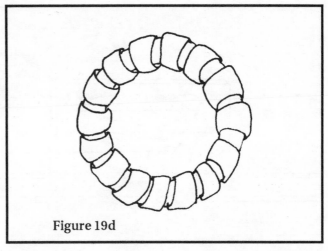

Figure 19d

should refer to it there. It necessitates the use of really advanced manipulative skills and should be used only when the craftworker is ready for a challenge. It does lend a piece a nice old look as very few modern quillworkers are willing to go to all of the bother and trouble of crafting a rosette with this technique.

Quillwork on Birch Bark

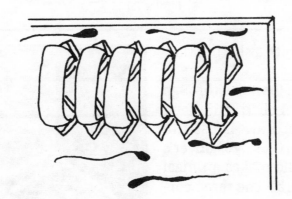

Quillwork done on birch bark requires no actual sewing during the quilling process, making this another technique ideally suited to the would be quillworker who lacks polish in sewing skills. The bark should be gathered when the sap is up in the tree and thinned by removing a few layers of the outer and inner bark (they separate easiest at this time) and

then laid out flat to dry. It is possible to flatten bark that has been allowed to dry curled by either soaking it in simmering water or steaming it and then laying it out flat to dry but this is fairly difficult and should be avoided if at all possible. The quillwork is done on the bark when it is wet, so after flattening it, the bark must be soaked again. The design to be quilled

71

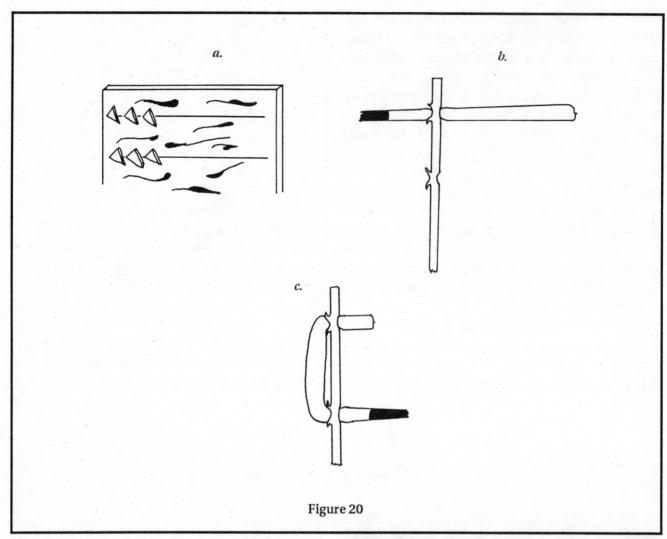

Figure 20

can be drawn on the back with a sharp scribe.

Figure 20a illustrates some of the holes, through which the quills will pass, punched in the bark. A very small, three cornered awl is used to make the holes. A Size 6/0 or 7/0 glover's needle mounted in a handle makes an ideal awl for this type of quillwork. The three cornered hole holds the quill securely and the small size allows the holes to be punched close enough together that when the bark drys the quills will not be spaced too far apart. A typical awl used for this work is shown in a photograph at the beginning of this book (see *Tools*).

A row of quillwork is formed by pushing an untrimmed quill through a hole along the top guideline, working from the back of the piece

to the front, and then pushing it through the corresponding hole along the bottom of the row from the front of the piece to the back as shown in Figure 20b and 20c. It will probably be necessary to pull the quill most of the way through the bark with a pair of needlenose pliers as a quill is not stiff enough to be pushed through such a small hole for its entire length.

Figure 20 shows only one method of laying quills on birch bark. There are a number of design elements available to the more imaginative quillworker. Quills may be criss-crossed and woven in and out of each other, and more than one quill can run through the punched holes at a time. With some thought, designs may incorporate different textures in the same project.

When the quillwork is finished, clip off the quill ends leaving approximately 1/4" or less on the back of the piece. The ends should be made to lay as flat as possible, and then a bark liner is sewn to the inside of the work with a whip stitch. Most often this will be the only sewing needed. If it is available, the bark should be sewn with spruce root but other fibers may also be used. Some pieces are sewn with sweet grass and others are sewn with sinew. Practically any natural fiber will work.

Loom Quillwork

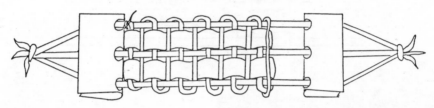

Loom quillwork is another technique that requires little in the way of sewing skills. Only general sewing will be needed to mount the finished piece on a foundation of leather or rawhide. To begin, a loom must be constructed. As can be seen in the photograph at the beginning of this section, it is a simple loom made of a bent stick of about an inch in diameter. It is possible to carve a really fine loom from straight grain woods, such as ash, but unless having such a fine tool makes a difference to the individual craftsman, a bent stick allows the work to proceed just fine. If one finds that working with a loom is truly enjoyable and a great deal of time is spent with loom quillwork, by all means carve one.

In loom quillwork it is necessary to plan out the design in advance. Because of the limitations imposed by this technique, the designs must be geometric. When the design is set, it will be possible to determine the number of warp threads to be strung on the loom. The warp threads are those that are tied to both

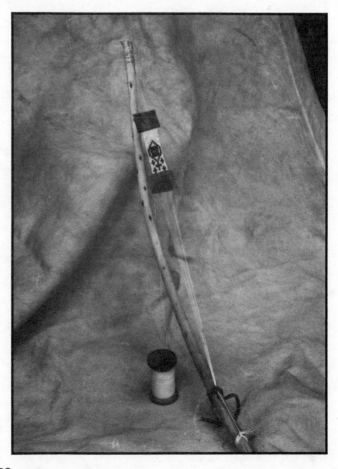

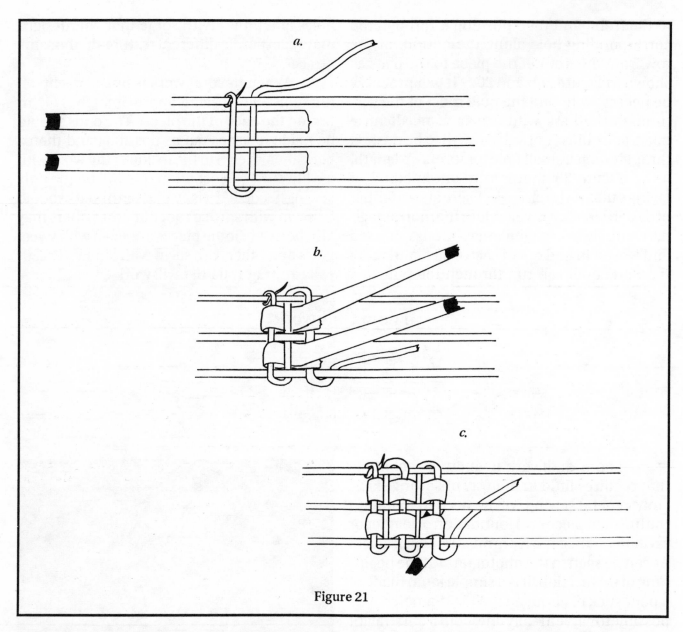

Figure 21

ends of the loom. Traditionally, the warp was made of either sinew or vegetable fiber but more recently cotton threads are used for both the warp and the weft (the thread that will do the weaving). Another option is the use of silk threads. The silk is slippery and lets the weft pack very tightly. A fairly heavy weight thread (about size F) works well.

Tie the desired number of threads to one end of the loom. The next step is to run each thread through the two spreaders; these can be made from either birch bark or rawhide. An example of the spreaders may be seen in the illustration at the beginning of this chapter. They are made of rectangles of bark or rawhide, folded in half with the correct number of holes punched a quills width apart. A medium size awl will give the proper sized hole. After the threads have been run through the holes, the edges of the rectangle can be lashed together to maintain a good fold. Tie off the loose warp threads to the other end of the loom. The loom is now set up and ready for the quillwork to begin.

The diagrams in Figure 21 demonstrate the techniques of loom quillwork. Tie the weft thread to either the far right or left warp thread with an over hand knot and lay out the initial quills as shown in illustration 21a. The quills are on the underside of the first row of weft. In illustration 21b, the quills are folded over the first weft row and placed under the second weft row. As may be seen in the same diagram, the third row of weft runs under both the working end of the quill and the follicle tip. This locks the first quill in place in the piece and the same principle is used throughout the entire work to lock in additional quills as they are spliced in. In 21c the work has continued to the ends of the first quills. They are shown bent to the underside of the piece. They will remain in this position until the piece is finished and then all of the ends will be clipped off to a uniform length. Once again, new quills are added to the work in the same manner that the first quills were locked in place.

In the illustrations, the quillwork is shown spread apart so that the reader can understand how the techniques are done. In reality, the quillwork should be kept as tight as possible; actually it is packed tightly together. This can be facilitated by using the bottom spreader as a packing tool. Simply slide it up the warp threads and push hard against the quillwork. In addition to giving the quillwork a nice finish, the packing keeps the splices firmly locked in place. When the piece is finished, wrap the weft threads around the bottom of

the work a few times to stabilize the last quills. The piece may then be removed from the loom and mounted on some foundation material. Leather will usually be the best for this purpose.

Repairing Damaged Quillwork

Experienced quillworkers are often asked to repair damaged quilled pieces. Occasionally, the repairs will be done on antique pieces and extreme caution must be used. More often, however, the piece will be more contemporary and the damage has been caused by abrasion or insects. Both kinds of damage are fairly easy to repair as long as the foundation is in good condition; this is the first thing that should be checked. If the quillwork is sewn on leather, as is usually the case, see if the leather is sound enough to hold new stitches by taking

a few tiny stitches in it and pulling them taut. If the stitches do not hold well, there is no point in proceeding with the repairs. The foundation must be sound.

If the piece passes the first test, the next step is to inventory the materials used in the quillwork and try to match them as closely as possible. The main difficulty will probably be matching the dyes of the quills. It is very nearly impossible to get an exact match, so be willing to settle for a shade lighter or darker. If there is no time pressure, the repair quills may be dyed

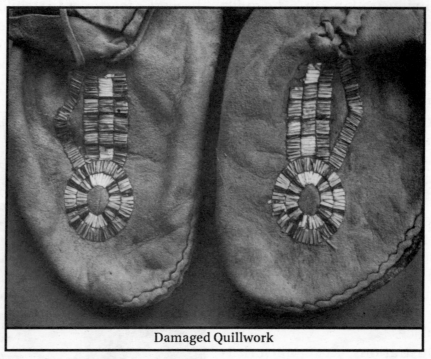
Damaged Quillwork

slightly darker and then set on a sunny window sill to fade naturally. Be sure to turn the quills every other day or so to allow them to fade evenly on all sides. This trick can be invaluable when trying to match modern dyes to the colors on older pieces which have faded from years of use. It is surprising how little time is required if the sunshine is strong and direct.

The techniques in this book should cover most of the repairs a quillworker will come across. Always practice a technique on a scrap of leather before working on the old piece. With some careful study it will be possible to identify idiosyncrasies within the original work and to adapt your style to match. No two quillworkers ever work exactly alike and identifying differences in methods is crucial to a sound replication of the techniques used in the original. When all is ready, simply snip the damaged quills out of the row, make a note of all color changes and their proper placement, and fill in the necessary spaces. Unless absolutely necessary, do not attempt to remove the old stitches. Digging them out of the leather may cause damage that will be difficult to quill over smoothly. Upon completing the repairs, burnish all of the quillwork, new and old, with a quill flattener. Older quillwork is often swelled from moisture and re-flattening it will help protect the work from further damage.

There is one more thing that a quillworker must learn: When asked to repair antique pieces, learn to say "No." In most cases, a piece is much more valuable, both monetarily and historically, if it is left as it is. Repairs should be restricted to stitching down loose quills and re-flattening, and occasionally glueing down an errant quill if it is impossible to stitch it properly.

APPENDIX A

THE PREPARATION OF RAWHIDE AND BRAIN TANNED LEATHER

As mentioned earlier in this book, it is essential for the serious quillworker to have a steady supply of good quality brain tanned leather. With the high cost of each hide, it is necessary for all but the most affluent quillworker to learn to tan their own. Master this skill early. It takes only slightly less time to learn than quillwork and by the time one is able to quill with some speed, there should be a ready supply of hides on which to work.

There are many different methods employed in brain tanning. This appendix will cover only one and will describe that as simply as possible. It shall be left to the more serious student of tanning to develop further skills. It is a fascinating study as every tanner seems to

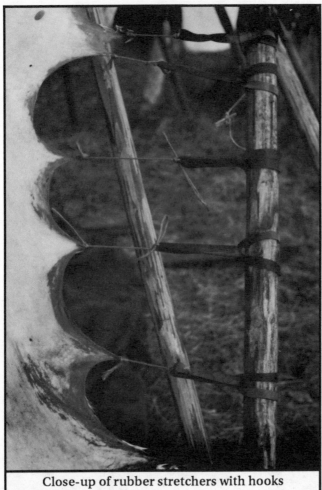

Close-up of rubber stretchers with hooks and ties.

Tanning equipment - beam, tool, rope and five gallon solution bucket

work in a different manner.

The photographs in this section show some of the necessary equipment for the procedure presented in this section. The fleshing and graining tool shown in the photo on Page 77 (left) is made from a planer blade. The hardness of the steel in the planer blade makes it the best fleshing and graining tool available. However, a simple draw knife also works well as a fleshing and graining tool and the smallest size available should be used. When fleshing and graining with this type of tool, keep the beveled side of the blade faced down. The same is true for a tool made from a planer blade. Any work knife that seems comfortable is suitable for the minor trimming needed in fleshing and graining hides. Keep it handy so that there is no temptation to trim and cut with the fleshing and graining tool as that must be

kept as sharp as possible.

A stretching frame is used to dry the hides (Photo on Page 77 - right). The stretching action keeps the hides flat and smooth as they dry and allows the hide enough movement so that the resulting rawhide is white with a fairly open texture. The frame may be made from lumber that is bolted together or it may be fashioned from round poles. The close-up photo of the hooks that are on the stretching frame (above left) show that they are mounted on short, rubber bands. The bands allow the stretching action that is required and are made by cutting up old inner tubes. String may be used to tie the hide to the rubber bands.

The Photo on Page 79 (top left) shows the tanning beam and breaking tool. The breaking tool is used to break open the hide fibers as the brain solution is worked into the hide. The

78

Tanning beam
and tool

Smoking equipment - Smoker,
blower and rotten wood

tanning beam may be made from any kind of lumber as long as the blade that the hide is stretched on is made from hardwood. A plastic rope, approximately 3/8" in diameter (not shown) will also be used in the stretching procedure. The addition of a clean canvas tarp under the work area assures that a white hide will remain white.

The essentials for smoking leather are shown in the Photo above (left side). There are many possibilities for the construction of smokers. A serviceable smoker may be made from two buckets. A five gallon steel bucket and a 2 1/2 gallon galvanized feed bucket may be placed, open ends together, with a six inch stove pipe coming out of the feed bucket. A strip of flashing, six inches wide, is then screwed on the wide end of the feed bucket so that when it is inverted over the steel fire bucket the flash-

ing will extend over the steel bucket and prevent excess air from entering the smudge chamber and fanning the coals into flames. Sometimes it is also necessary to place stove putty in the crack around the stove pipe for the same reason. This style of smoker will not be prone to catching fire as the hides are smoked, but it may be difficult to build up a bed of coals. It may be necessary, therefore, to have something on hand with which to blow air on the fire. A blacksmith's hand cranked forge blower works quite well but if this proves difficult to find, a set of bellows is easy to make.

Additional supplies that have to be obtained are brains and fabric softener (the tanner's secret weapon). In the latter, Downey seems to be the brand that works best. Also, a seven (7') foot length of 4" plastic pipe will be used as a beam for fleshing and graining.

Fleshing and Graining

In the process of turning green (unprocessed) hides into leather or rawhide, the meat and membrane must be removed from one side of the hide and the hair and upper epidermis must be removed from the other. The former task is referred to as "fleshing the hide," and the latter is "graining the hide." The side of the hide that is fleshed is referred to as the *flesh side* and the side from which the hair and upper epidermis is removed, or grained, is called the *grain side* of the hide. The grain side (or top of the hide) is the side which shows when the leather is formed into a usable object. It is therefore considered to be a bit more important and the utmost care should be exercised when working on this side.

To begin, soak the hide thoroughly in water. A plastic garbage can is ideally suited, but any container may be used. Drape the soaked hide, hair (grain) side down, across the fleshing beam. Always flesh the hides first. Aside from removing the rancid flesh and fat and allowing the second soaking to clean the hide somewhat, the hair on the underside will pad this part of the work. The padding will prevent the tools from puncturing the hide in the more difficult areas.

It is easiest to flesh a hide by working from the neck down toward the tail. Place the fleshing tool against the hide, beveled side down, and scrape the meat and membrane off the hide with a slightly diagonal scraping motion. If the hide is completely soaked through, this step should move along at a fairly rapid rate. It may take longer at first, but as confidence and skill are gained a hide will usually be fleshed in forty-five minutes or less. Be extra careful as the work moves along the flanks of the animal; this area is very thin and it is easy to punch holes through the hide. Sometimes the flanks are so weak that it is best to trim out the worst of it. When the fleshing is finished, return the hide to the container and allow it to soak once more. If it soaks overnight, the hide will swell with water and the next step will be easier. This also lets the tanner rest. Actually, if fleshing an entire hide seems too much at first, there is no reason not to split the fleshing and graining into four sessions instead of two. Be sure, however, that the hide does not begin to rot. Frequent changing of the water will extend the amount of time that the hide can be soaked.

Graining the hide is done in the same way as fleshing. Work from the neck down using short, diagonal strokes. Carefully examine the area covered by each stroke and insure that the epidermis is completely removed. Failure to remove the grain completely will result in visible streaks on a finished white hide, and in major flaws on smoked leather. At first it will be difficult to be sure, but with practice the eyes will grow accustomed to seeing any spots that have been skipped. Don't despair if the first few hides are less than perfect.

When both the fleshing and graining are complete, mount the hide in the stretching frame to dry. Allow it to remain in the frame for several days so that the hide fibers will be opened to some extent by the pulling exerted by the rubber bands. This initial opening will facilitate an easier tanning procedure. Working the hides in winter will aid in this as the freezing will open the hide fibers a great deal. If the tanner lives in an area where no freezing occurs, it is possible to accomplish the same thing by using a round blade of some sort (an axe head works well) to squeeze excess water out of the hide by rubbing the blade firmly down the hide while it is stretched in the frame. Then, as the hide dries, rub it several more times with the blade working up and down the hide and across the hide also. The result should be a fairly flexible, white rawhide. After the hide is taken from the frame, it may be rolled and stored.

Tanning

In the brain tanning process, the brain solution permeates the hide and allows the fibers of the hide to remain open as the tanner stretches the drying hide. One of the challenges in this process, therefore, is to work a sufficient amount of brains into the hide to get everything going smoothly. Mix the solution in a five gallon, plastic pail. There is enough room in a container of this size to allow several hides to be worked at the same time. When first tanning, one hide is plenty of work, but as the procedure becomes more familiar, it is possible to tan three or four hides at the same time. An added advantage of this is the maximum use of each batch of brain solution.

Prepare the solution by either crushing or blending about two quarts of brains and mixing it with enough water to make a thick sludge. Simmer this for twenty minutes, taking care that it does not stick to the bottom of the pan. It should not actually boil. Place about three gallons of hot water in the plastic pail, add the brains and stir. Add half a cap of fabric softener to the solution and swish it around with your hand. If you cannot leave your hand in the solution for a slow count of ten, it is too warm and should be given time to cool before the hides are submerged.

Start soaking the hides in the solution the evening before the tanning is to be done. Place the dried hides in the warm solution and slowly work them under the surface; then place a weight on them to keep them submerged over night. Early the next morning, drain the brain solution into a pot to re-heat and take the partially soaked hides out to the fleshing and graining beam. The fibers of the hides may be broken open a little bit more by lightly scraping across the hide with a breaking tool. **Photo 48** (Page 79 - top left) illustrates one such tool; it is essentially a straight metal edge with wooden handles. If the fleshing and graining were done with a draw knife, the back edge of that tool will work fine. The one in the photograph is made from a worn-out hoof rasp with one edge ground smooth, but just about any straight metal edge will work. Dragging the tool across the hide will cause the fibers to open and this lets the brain solution penetrate deeper into the hide. On thin hides it will only be necessary to perform the breaking one time, but on thicker hides it may take two or three times. Return the hides to the warm brain solution after each breaking and let them soak for at least an hour. When it seems that the brain solution has fully penetrated the hides, work them over with your hands. Pull and stretch every inch of the hides to check for any small, hard spots. Work these places out by repeatedly dipping them in the solution and flexing them by hand. Keep the brain solution warm during this entire period as it will penetrate the hides faster and more completely than will a cooled solution. When the hide is thoroughly wet and totally pliable, wring and squeeze out excess moisture and hang the hide to dry. Wring only enough solution out of the hide so that it doesn't drip. It is hard work to get all of the brain solution into the hide and it would be counter productive to remove too much.

Rawhide

At this point the hide may be stretched and dried for rawhide. Simply hang it in the stretching frame for several days in the shade. Rawhide that has been brained is a pliable, white material that makes it easy to work with and has a nice open texture. The texture may be opened even further by rubbing the axe head over the hide as it dries.

Leather

As the hides dry, the actual tanning can begin. Notice how the hides stiffen as they dry. A tanner's main concern is to keep the stiffness worked out of the hides and to do this, the wooden tanning beam and plastic tanning rope

The author working an elk hide on the rope. A session on the beam will follow.

regaining a stretchy relaxed feeling, again hang it to dry (See Photo below). As it begins to tighten once more, take it down and work through it. Repeat this several times and slowly add in some work on the tanning beam by rubbing the flesh side of the hide against the blade on the beam; it is always necessary to follow the beam work with some rope work. The beam tends to tighten the hide fibers while the hide is still fairly damp and the rope will help to relax the tightness. There is, however, a point at which the hide is ready to be worked entirely on the beam. This is when the hide is about two-thirds dry. Suddenly the rope will start to leave wrinkles and creases and the beam will no longer tighten the fibers. Beam the hide on the flesh side to start and then work it on both sides as the hide gets closer to being dry.

About midway in the drying process, it will also become easier to pass a needle through

are used. As a rule, the rope will be used to work the hides at their wettest stages and the beam after the hides dry enough to have gained some of their fluffy loft. However, in actual practice, both pieces of equipment are used throughout the entire procedure. The rope is tied off as shown in the Photo above, and then the hide is worked on it by grasping the hide firmly in both hands and pulling it against the rope and rubbing it back and forth. The grain side of the hide should be against the rope. Develop a technique in rubbing so that the entire hide is stretched in all directions: Work first from the tail to the neck, stretching the hide across its width, and then work from one side to the other stretching the hide from tail to neck. It is also good to work the hide diagonally. Be sure that as the work proceeds that the edges are also kept pliable.

After working through the hide and

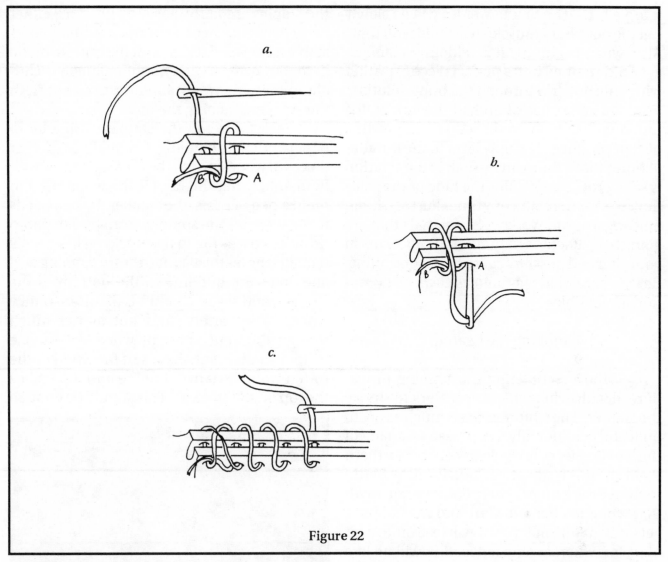

Figure 22

the hide and this is when any holes should be sewn closed. By using a fine needle and thread, it is possible to do this so that the holes will be hardly noticeable. A Size 12 sharps needle (the same size that is used for quillwork) and Size A Nymo Thread will work very well. As shown in Figure 22, use a double thickness of the thread and whip stitch the trimmed edges of the hole together on the flesh side of the hide. In Illustration 22a the thread is knotted on the leather by stitching through both thicknesses of the leather at Point A. Pass the needle and thread through the leather and another stitch is taken at Point B. Be sure that this stitch catches the end of the thread as shown in the diagram. Illustration 22a shows only one back stitch taken over the end of the thread, but for extra security two or more may be added. In 22b the needle again passes through Point A locking the previous stitches in place and completing the knot. Continue to stitch along the edge of the hole as shown in Illustration 22c. When the hole is closed, stitch back two or three times to secure the end of the thread once more. Try to make all of the stitches as small as possible. If the holes are sewn early enough in the tanning procedure the subsequent stretching should pull out all of the puckers caused by sewing the hole closed.

If at any time during tanning one begins to tire, discontinue working, wrap the hide in a plastic bag and store it in the freezer; a refrigerator will serve to store a hide over night. It is best to work on leather when one is able to give it top effort. The first few hides will go slowly but the necessary muscles will build with time. Also, when beginning it is seldom possible to get a hide tanned into a perfect piece of leather with only one trip through the brain solution. Even an expert has often had to work brains into hides up to three times to end up with a decent product. The only limit to the number of times that a hide can re-soak in the solution is set by rot. Never allow the hide or the solution to start to smell at any time. Further, it can be dangerous to work with materials that are going bad. Bacteria may enter through cuts in your skin and possibly cause blood poisoning. Be very careful to maintain as clean an operation as possible.

Smoking the Leather

Upon completing the tanning procedure, decide whether it is necessary to smoke the leather. The white leather is much easier to quill and traditionally it was used for many of the fancier pieces of quillwork on the northern Plains. If this is not important, it will be better to smoke the leather. There is a common myth that white leather will turn into rawhide if it gets wet. While not true, it will lose quite a bit of its loft whereas smoked leather will be less affected by such neglect. Also, quillwork is often more striking on a dark background. It is generally a matter of personal preference, but if the plan is to sell the work, pieces on smoked leather often sell faster.

The best methods for smoking force the smoke through the leather, completely permeating every fiber. The smoker shown in the Photograph on Page 79 (right) will accomplish this very well. To use it, the hide must be sewn into a "bag" with the grain side in. First, trim away any edges that are hard or ragged. Then, fold the hide in half lengthwise and stitch from the tail towards to neck. A sewing machine with a fine needle and polyester thread works well. The hide may, if a sewing machine is not available, be stapled together but be sure that

the staples are fairly close together. In either case, leave the neck area open and stitch or staple a canvas extension on the bottom of the hide. An extension of about eighteen inches eliminates any worry about excess heat from the smoker reaching the hide.

Start a fire in the smoker with a lot of paper and small kindling. Gradually add larger pieces of wood and fan the fire with the blower. Remember that the harder the wood used to build a bed of coals, the smaller the bed needs to be. Prevent the smudge from bursting into fire at all cost as fire in the smoker will severely damage the leather. When the fire is going well and coals are building in the bottom of the smoker, add several handfuls of rotten, punky wood. The variety does not matter much though different kinds of wood will smoke leather to different shades of brown. Let the rotten wood heat over the fire and then place the top on the smoker. This should be enough

to smother the flames and create a thick smoke. If not, place something over the stove pipe and seal off all of the air. A shovel or some flat piece of metal works fine.

Suspend the hide over the smoker so that the canvas extension drapes over the stove pipe and tie a rope around it to prevent smoke from escaping out the bottom. A tipi makes the perfect shelter in which to smoke leather. It is easy to run a rope nine or ten feet off the ground and suspend the hide from it while protecting the leather from the wind; too much wind can prevent an even smoking. The Photo on Page 84 shows a smoker in operation. The canvas has been removed from the tipi so that it is possible to see the entire setup. The strings that hold the hide in suspension are fastened to the leather with safety pins.

With the proper smudge, the smoking does not take very long. On thinner hides, ten minutes is all that is usually required on each side. The thickest leather seldom takes longer than twenty-five minutes per side. Some people smoke only the grain side of the leather but the smoke will have better penetration if the hide is removed from the smoker when the desired color is reached on the grain side, turned inside out and returned to the smoker so that the flesh side is also smoked. When the smoking is finished, break open the stitching so that the hide is again flat. Then remove the canvas from the bottom and hang the finished leather out on a line to air and cure. It is possible to let the hide hang for several days to dissipate the smokey smell, but it must be taken in at night to keep it from becoming damp.

APPENDIX B

Old Time Dyes for Porcupine Quills

When Native American cultures ran headlong into the invading European cultures many things changed at a rapid rate. The indigenous Tribes began to absorb technology from distant lands and to lay aside aspects of their centuries old traditions; many areas of learning were deemed no longer necessary and were quickly forgotten. This was the way with the art of producing brilliant quill dyes from locally available plants and mineral materials. Even as early as the 1830s, Maximillian commented on this loss as natives turned to European traders for goods from which dyes could be rendered. In some cases, dyes were actually traded for and in others the dyes were removed from cloth and blankets. In any event, the loss of expertise in this area has been almost irretrievable. Very little was ever recorded on the subject and the slim gleanings serve only to tantalize.

The following lists have been compiled from years of research on the subject and quite a lot of personal experimentation. Most of the experiments were failures but there are still quite a few combinations needing to be tried. When experimenting with some combinations, use a great deal of caution. Do not place quills, that have been dyed with various minerals and/ or questionable plant substances, in the mouth to soak before using them for sewing. It is better to keep them damp in a moistened paper towel . . . just in case.

General Dye Plant List

Red

1. Blood root - *Sanguinaria canadensis*
2. Sassafrass - *Sassafras albidum*
3. Red Bedstraw - *Galium tinctorium*
4. Alder - *Alnus rubra and incana*
5. Buffalo berry - *Lepargyrea*
6. Puccoon - *Lithospermum carolinense*
7. Red Osier Dogwood - *Cornus stolonifera*
8. Wild Plum or Chokecherry - *Prunus americanus*
9. Hemlock - *Tsuga canadensis*
10. Red Cedar - *Juniperus virginiana*

Yellow

1. Cottonwood - *Populus sargentil*
2. Smooth Sumac - *Rhus glabra*
3. Lichen - *Usnea barbata*
4. Gold thread - *Helleborus trifolis*
5. Oregon Grape - *Berberis repens*
6. Sunflower - *Retibida columifera*
7. Fox Moss - *Evernia vulpina*
8. Curled Dock - *Rumex crispus*
9. Osage Orange - *Maclura pomifera*

Black

1. Walnut - *Juglan nigra*
2. Maples - *Acre* (most varieties)
3. Wild Grape - *Vitis, cinera* and *vulpina*
4. Hickory - *Hicoria ovata*
5. Burr Oak - *Quercus macrocarpa*
6. Elder berries - *Sambucus melanocarpa*

Brown
1. Rushes - *Juncus belticus*

Purple
1. Elder berries - *Sambucus melanocarpa*
2. Northern Dog Whelk - *Nucella lapillus*
3. Blackberries - *Rubus ursinus*
4. White Maple - *Acer* variety unknown

Green
1. Prince's Pine - *Chimiphila umbellata*
2. Moosewood - no taxonomic information available
3. Evergreen - *Arbutus menziesa*

Blue
1. Beech - *Fagus*
2. Wire Birch - possibly *Betula lenta*
3. Larkspur - *Delphinium nelsoni*

General Mordant List

1. Birch - all varieties.
2. Oak - all varieties, but black oak is best.
3. Iron oxides - made by soaking pieces of iron in acidic solutions for several weeks.
4. Nut Galls - galls found on species of oak trees; they contain concentrations of tannic acid.
5. Sumac - *Rhus glabra*, contains about 25% tannin
6. Alder - *Alnus rubra* and *incana*.
7. Black Oak - this is allowed to set in stagnant water for two years and then ground to a dust which is the mordant; this being full of iron. It is similar in makeup to grindstone dust in common use among vegetable dyers.
8. Ashes - most often hardwood ashes are used; but, sometimes cedar bark ashes are needed.
9. Allum - when in doubt as to how to strengthen a dye, add allum.
10. Vinegar - while this is not a true mordant, it is listed here as an aid in dying. Small amounts can be added to the dye water and this will help the colors remain true and penetrate the quills in many cases.
11. Dock - *Rumex*, the roots of the female plants.

Dye Formulas

The following list of formulas is by no means complete. Some of them are combinations worked out by the author and others were recorded by some early ethno-botanists. Prominent among these stand the works of Frances Densmore and W.D. Wallis.

Red
1. Blood root and alder inner bark mixed in equal parts and boiled in water. Add allum. Simmer quills in resulting liquid until desired shade is reached.
2. Two parts of blood root, one part alder, one part red osier dogwood, one part choke cherry. Boil for quite awhile and then steep quills in the hot liquid.
3. Nine inches of puccoon root boiled in one quart of water. Soak quills in hot water and then simmer in dye for half an hour and let set overnight. May be re-dyed to get desired shade.
4. Scrape the outer bark off of hemlock root and boil the rest with allum added. Soak the quills in the hot liquid. Grindstone dust may be used instead of the allum.
5. Boil the bark from oak, white birch and red osier dogwood. Add two cups of cedar bark ash to the liquid and boil again. Strain the liquid and add previously soaked quills.
6. Buffalo berry or squaw currents boiled in water with female dock root. Steep quills in hot dye bath. Allum may be added.
7. Red bedstraw boiled in water with allum. Quills are steeped in the dye bath. Re-dye the quills until the desired shade is reached.

Yellow
1. Boil the roots of Oregon grape and the petals of sunflowers in water with either allum or dock root added. Steep the quills in the resulting dye bath. Re-dye until the desired

shade is obtained.

2. Pulverize sumac stalk and boil with female dock root. Simmer quills in resulting dye bath.

3. Boil together shredded sumac, shredded choke cherry root, pounded bloodroot and shredded alder bark. Add allum to aid in setting the color and then steep the quills taking care to keep the solution hot.

4. Pound fox or wolf moss and boil with the quills.

5. Boil cottonwood leaf buds with female dock root and simmer the quills in the dye bath. Re-dye to get the desired shade.

6. Gather a lot of goldthread roots (these are very slender and many are required) and boil with either allum or female dock root. Simmer the quills in the dye bath.

Black

1. Sprinkle walnut hulls with water until they turn black. Then boil them with allum and steep the quills in the dye bath which is kept very hot.

2. Boil a lot of wild grape with the walnut hulls as prepared above. Steep the quills in the hot dye bath. Grindstone dust may be added to the dye bath also.

3. Boil alder and red osier dogwood and oak with grindstone dust or black earth containing iron compounds. Simmer quills in the dye bath.

4. Boil rotten (very rotten) maple with oxidized iron and sumac. Simmer the quills in the dye bath and re-dye until the desired shade is obtained.

5. Boil white maple and elm together with oxidized iron and sumac. Simmer the quills in the dye bath and re-dye as necessary.

6. Boil maple with hardwood ashes. Strain the dye bath and simmer the quills in the dye.

7. Try adding elder berries to any of the above recipes.

Brown

1. Boil hemlock roots with alder and simmer the quills in the dye bath. Re-dye to obtain the desired shade.

2. Boil rushes with iron or oxidized iron. Steep the quills in the dye bath.

3. Boil moss found growing in the cracks of maple bark with the quills. Oxidized iron may strengthen the dye.

Purple

1. Rotten maple and grindstone dust boiled with the quills.

2. Blackberries boiled with either female dock root or allum. The quills are steeped in the dye bath which is kept hot. Re-dye to obtain the proper shade.

3. Boil northern dog whelk with elder berries and the quills.

Green

1. Boil urine and copper together. The more it is boiled down, the stronger the dye. Steep quills in the dye bath and re-dye as necessary.

2. Boil moosewood for about an hour. Take it out and crush and then re-boil with allum. Steep the quills in hot dye bath.

3. Boil the inner green bark of an evergreen (arbutus menziesa). Add allum and steep the quills in the hot solution.

Blue

1. Boil the bark of the beech and add a gallon of water to which has been added a tablespoon of hardwood ashes. Simmer the quills in the dye bath and re-dye as needed.

2. Boil urine and copper together. The procedure and recipe are the same as those presented in the green category. The difference being in the urine. Sometimes blue will be the result, sometimes green.

3. Boil wire birch and add female dock root. Simmer quills in the dye bath.

4. Boil larkspur flowers with allum and steep the quills in the very hot dye bath. Re-dye.

BIBLIOGRAPHY

Androska, Rita J. *Natural Dyes and Home Dying*, 1971, Dover Publications, New York

Bebbington, Julia M. *Quillwork of the Plains*, Glenbow Museum, Calgary, Alberta

Brasser, Ted J. *"Bo'jou, Neejee!" Profiles of Canadian Indian Art*, 1976, Museum of Man, Ottawa, Ontario

Coe, Ralph T. *Sacred Circles: Two Thousand Years of North American Indian Art*, 1976, Arts Council of Great Britain

Conn, Richard. *Native American Art in the Denver Art Museum*, 1979, Denver Art Museum

Densmore, Frances. *How Indians Use Wild Plants for Food, Medicine and Crafts*, 1974, Dover Publications, New York

Flint Institute of Arts. *Art of the Great Lakes Indians*, 1973, Flint Institute of Arts, Flint, Michigan

Gilmore, Melvin R. *Uses of Plants by the Indians of the Missouri River Region*, 1977, University of Nebraska Press, Lincoln, Nebraska

Hart, Jeff. *Montana: Native Plants and Early Peoples*, 1976, Montana Historical Society, Helena, Montana

Lesch, Alma. *Vegetable Dyeing*, 1970, Watson-Guptill Publications, New York

Marrow, Mable. *Indian Rawhide: An American Folk Art*, 1975, University of Oklahoma, Norman, Oklahoma

Orchard, William C. *The Technique of Porcupine Quill Decoration Among the Indians of North America*, 1984, Eagle's View Publishing, Liberty, Utah

Thomas, Davis and Ronnefeldt, Karin. *People of the First Man: Life Among the Plains Indians in Their Final Days of Glory, First hand Account of the Prince Maximillian Expedition 1833-34*, 1976, E.P. Dutton and Company, Inc. New York

Whitehead, Ruth Holmes. *Micmac Quillwork*, 1982, Nova Scotia Museum, Halifax, Nova Scotia

Museum Collections of Notes

Buffalo Bill Cody Museum, Cody, Wyoming

Coulter Bay Indian Museum, Yellowstone National Park, Wyoming

Denver Art Museum, Denver, Colorado

The Field Museum of Natural History, Chicago

Glenbow Museum, Calgary, Alberta

Joslyn Art Museum, Omaha, Nebraska

Linden Museum, Stuttgart, West Germany

Manitoba Museum of Man and Nature, Winnipeg, Manitoba

Museum of the American Indian, Heye Foundation, New York

National Museum of Denmark, Dept of Ethnology, Coppenhaggen

National Museum of Man, Ottawa, Ontario

National Museum of Natural History, Smithsonian, Washington DC

The Royal Scottish Museum, United Kingdom

The Visitors of the Ashmolean Museum, Oxford

AMERICA'S *FIRST*
FIRST WORLD WAR:

The French and Indian War, 1754-1763
by Timothy J. Todish

AMERICA'S *FIRST* FIRST WORLD WAR:
The French & Indian War, 1754-1763
by
Timothy J. Todish

An excellent illustrated summary of one of the most important eras in the history of North America. The author explains the roles played by the French, the British, the Indian allies on both sides, and by the Colonials with warranted emphasis on Robert Rogers and his Rangers. The importance of the War to future governmental institutions, and social and economic patterns in North America, is made evident by the author in a style that is both informative and entertaining.

"Like Rogers, this author (like many recreators) sees straight to the heart of the matter. And this author is much more readable by today's standards than Rogers. A book by a recreator, for fellow recreators - a splendid capsule of America's first, First World War."
Living History Magazine

"Anyone who is interested in the French and Indian War would do well to order a copy of Timothy J. Todish's new book . . ."
Muzzleblasts Magazine

ETIENNE PROVOST
Man of the Mountains
by
Jack B. Tykal

The events of (Provost's) life represent a looking glass into the total history of the Rocky Mountain fur trade. It would have been very difficult to find a person closely associated with the beaver trade in the American west who did not only know Etienne, but considered him one of the outstanding individuals of that era. From Santa Fe and Taos to the remote valleys of the Rocky Mountains and the executive offices of the giant fur companies in St. Louis, his name was known and recognized as one who knew and understood every facet of the business. Whether trading with Ute Indians in the Great Basin, escaping the treachery of an ambush planned by Shoshone on a remote River which bore his name on early maps, or attending the first rendezvous with William Ashley in 1825, his services were recognized as invaluable.

Etienne Provost: Man of the Mountains reveals the life and adventures of this giant among fur trade personalities and is a welcome addition to the understanding of this remarkable era of the American West.
Dr. Fred Gowans

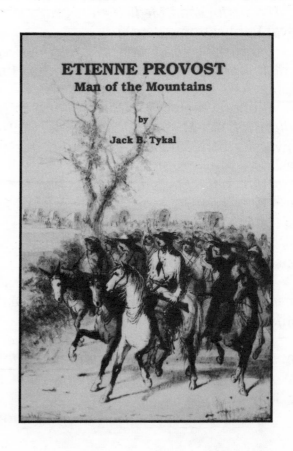

ETIENNE PROVOST
Man of the Mountains

by

Jack B. Tykal

NORTH AMERICAN BURIAL CUSTOMS
by
Dr. H. C. Yarrow

The mortuary customs of all of the major Indian Nations are explored and described in explicit verbage and with first-hand authority. Of import is that the contributors are very candid about any personal bias; a refreshing change from the position of contemporary social scientists with their claim of "objectivity" and emotional distance.

This informative and interesting book was written for the Smithsonian Institute in 1879 while Dr. Yarrow was serving as the acting surgeon general of the United States. Based on all available primary sources and personal research by physicians in the field, the book describes and illustrates in great detail all customs, including inhumatio, deposition, surface burial, cremation, aerial sepulture, aquatic burial and all of the ceremonies pertaining to these practices.

This book will be invaluable to anyone interested in the traditions and culture of the American Indian. It is well researched and makes fascinating reading.

NEW ADVENTURES IN BEADING EARRINGS
by
Laura Reid

This fantastic new book is fully illustrated and presents step-by-step instructions on making truly beautiful and distinctive earrings.

Written by noted craftsperson and author Laura Reid, each step is fully explained and the entire text has been "reader tested" and enthusiastically endorsed.

The styles include five-star, snowflake and cross point-style earrings; small fan, large bugle fan, large and small bugle fan, porcupine quill fan and circle fan-style earrings; and, three-square, bugle star in circle, large bugle rectangle, small bugle base, five bugle base, seven bugle base, ten bugle base and one dimensional cube square-type earrings.

All of the materials used are easily obtainable and all of the styles are based on seed beads and bugle beads. Further, from the styles explained and illustrated, and based on the easy-to-follow instructions, the reader is encouraged to go beyond the basics of the book and create their own designs.

Anyone who enjoys creating and then wearing beautiful craftwork will find this book to be a must.